DEB

DEAR JOHN

Through her own recollections and John's correspondence to her, Joan Le Mesurier describes how she first met John, then a successful stage actor who was unhappily married to Hattie Jacques. It was Hattie – a wonderful woman and lifelong friend – who encouraged Joan and John's relationship. Their marriage lasted twenty-one years and survived Joan's love affair with Tony Hancock. Joan gives the reader an insight into a remarkable life, taking us with her behind the scenes on many films as well as the hugely popular *Dad's Army* and into the world of their friendship with Peter Sellers, the Beatles and publicist Derek Taylor.

DEAR JOHN

DEAR JOHN

by

Joan Le Mesurier

Magna Large Print Books
Long Preston, North Yorkshire,
BD23 4ND, England.

British Library Cataloguing in Publication Data.

Le Mesurier, Joan
    Dear John.

    A catalogue record of this book is
    available from the British Library

    ISBN   0-7505-1936-3

First published in Great Britain in 2001 by Sidgwick & Jackson
an imprint of Macmillan Publishers Ltd.

Published in Large Print 2002 by arrangement with
Macmillan Publishers Ltd.

Magna Large Print is an imprint of Library Magna Books Ltd.

Printed and bound in Great Britain by
T.J. (International) Ltd., Cornwall, PL28 8RW

With thanks to Clive Dunn for permission to reproduce his poem, Joan Taylor for permission to reproduce Derek Taylor's letters, the Estates of Sir Alec Guinness and Peter Sellers for permission to reproduce their letters.

I dedicate this book to my dear John, and to all the people who wrote to him over the years, with a special kiss to the memory of Derek Taylor. Also to my family and friends whose love and support is my greatest blessing.

1

JOHN LE MESURIER
Beloved Actor
Born 5th April 1912
Died 16 November 1983

'Resting'

Between and beneath and beyond and above that short epitaph on a gravestone in St George's churchyard in Ramsgate, Kent, is the story of a quietly good and kind yet notable life. That of a gentleman in the broadest and truest sense, one whose life was characterized by a modest, kindly intensity and quite without the wasteful emotions of malice and greed.

To John Le Mesurier, my patient husband and friend, money and possessions meant very little. Friends, cricket, horses, dogs, cats, and music could all affect him. He could blub while watching a test match on TV. Being sentimental is not a crime although the ignorant may suggest that it is a sign of weakness. Sometimes it takes courage to weep.

John also loved his work, never losing a sense of bewilderment and wonder that he was being paid to do something he enjoyed so much. This is not to suggest that his art was as effortless as it seemed: that was the trick of it, as it is with most distinguished performers. Often, learning lines, dealing with less dedicated actors and similar demands scared the daylights out of him; but his calm and affable manner, onstage and off, was seldom shaken and throughout his life as a 'jobbing actor' (as he described himself with no false modesty whatsoever), they also often thrilled him. At times he would gain wry pleasure from the sheer absurdity of some of the things he was asked to do on stage or screen but which he would none the less accomplish with the flawless craft of the professional. And as a professional he wasn't above occasionally taking on daft work simply for the lolly. He was generous towards other actors and was often moved to tears by their performances, sometimes writing in congratulation if he had been particularly affected or amused. He was always mildly surprised and very touched when he received similar notes of praise.

A few years ago I wrote a book called *Lady Don't Fall Backwards* about my intense and passionate relationship with Tony Hancock, John's best friend. The affair began within months of my marriage and I described it with a curious mixture of shame, pain and joy. It all but destroyed our marriage. When Tony died in 1968 I was in splinters but, with extraordinary grace, John – who was in deep grief too, as I all but forgot – held out his arms to welcome me home and we resumed a married life that was characterized by an ever-deepening affection and trust. Writing that first book served to get Tony off my chest, so to speak. They were both dead by then and I had run away to live in Spain where I stayed for a few very healing years. But I have since wondered whether I failed to honour John enough in that earlier work. So this book is my letter to a beloved husband, dealing, I hope, with a few scraps of unfinished business. Dear John, I owe you one.

He wrote to me all the time – whenever he was away, even if it was only for a day or two. Notes scribbled on hotel writing paper, postcards, sometimes longer letters written during breaks from theatre, filming or TV schedules. I seldom replied in writing, being a telephone girl myself. I was also, quite simply, ashamed of my atrocious handwriting. So here, belatedly, I'm attempting to send him the long-stored, long-overdue answer. Of course, John also wrote to many other people and the gift of being a good correspondent means that sometimes brilliant letters come back in return. Some of those are included here.

And so this book came about, as I believe that letters reveal a person's true nature more clearly than anything else.

John's was a family who seldom expressed their feelings in the presence of others; it was considered bad form, a weakness. In my family, by contrast, emotions were volatile and easily roused; none of us was ever able to hide joy, sorrow or irritation for long. This is not to say that one way is better or healthier than the other – just that while I was brought up to blurt out just what I felt the moment the thought occurred to me, however idiotic it might be, John was constrained to be more thoughtful and sometimes to express his deepest feelings in writing or in some wry, apparently casual remark.

In John's letters I can see the full man and

in the letters he received from friends and acquaintances over the years, I see again the love and affection that they felt for him. Far from being a bloodlessly unemotional man, shackled by the curse of perfect manners, he could be as prone to irritations, depressions, doubts and even despair as the rest of us. It is simply that John conveyed such moods and responses with a mild irony, a shrug or gentle sarcasm often too subtle for everyone to catch. When pressed or stressed he could say the most damning things without the offender quite realizing that they had been sideswiped. In the main, however, he abominated confrontation of any kind and so deplored verbal, let alone physical, aggression that he took the lofty view that life was too short to get exercised about this or that tiresome little matter.

He was born on 5 April 1912 in the then pretty but nevertheless dull little town of Bedford, neither Home Counties, nor quite the industrial heartlands of England and notable only for a regatta which the locals regarded as second only to Henley and a fierce statue of the town's only other distinguished son, John Bunyan. The pilgrim progressed and John may well have been more spiritually attuned to Bury St

Edmunds, where he was raised. In this country town near Cambridge and Newmarket he was later to support the racing economy with his overgenerous backing of tired horses.

The family on his mother's side originated from Alderney in the Channel Islands, and were quite grand with a lineage, which went back to the tenth century and was dotted with titles. His birth name was John Charles Elton Le Mesurier De Somerys Hallilay the latter being his father's name which he later dropped, not through animosity but because of his desire to keep the Le Mesurier name going.

His childhood could not have contrasted more sharply with mine. John's was spent in a Queen Anne house with a paddock and tennis court in the grounds and, inside, servants, a library and a drawing-room with a grand piano. Mine was spent in a series of modest homes. Mum and Dad, Fred and Eleanor Long, did their best, I know, for me and my brothers, David and Terry, but they were always financially stretched so the family seldom had the money to foster the kind of hopes or ambitions that would encourage us kids to aspire to anything beyond their way of life. As carnival workers we had to move to wherever the work could be found and most of our homes not only lacked a drawing-room with a grand piano, but a bathroom and indoor lavatory as well. Instead, we had a potty under the bed and bathed once a week in a tin tub in front of the fire. And between proper soaks we had chilly all-over washes in the scullery.

My refuges from this respectable but terribly drab poverty were the local fleapit cinema and the public library. For me to imagine living in a house with its own library would have been beyond any dream or fantasy. And to John as a child, my life would have seemed equally bewildering. Nevertheless we both had security in loving homes, for while John was affectionately reared by a nanny, I had Grandma. It wasn't that our parents didn't care for us but his nanny and my granny gave each of us something extra.

However, although John lived in a genteel and rural community where the outside world was seldom allowed to intrude, when this did happen it made him prick up his ears and ask questions. He never forgot an occasion when he and his nanny passed a striking group of people in Bury High Street: the men wore large black hats and long overcoats with astrakhan collars; the ladies were flamboyant, probably over-dressed and wore lots of make-up. When he asked the nanny who they were she replied, 'They are theatricals, Master John, and you must have nothing to do with them.'

Despite nanny's admonishments, or per-haps because of them, something took a grip. John loved the circus and was filled with wonderment about the people who lived in the painted wagons which some-times rumbled through the streets of his peaceful town in a clamour of noise and colour then mysteriously disappeared over-night, leaving only a flattened circle where the big ring had been. An aching curiosity formed about a world that was light years away from his own and he tended to retreat into his imaginary world. He had an older sister, Michelle, but never got to know her very well. He says in his autobiography that the fault was probably his: he was not easy to grow up with. There were many occa-sions, he said, when he was sullen and incoherently demanding: the typical beha-viour of the younger, slightly spoilt child. Michelle was popular and had many accomplishments, such as riding, playing tennis and flirting. She married, John told me, a rather humourless army officer who had a curious moustache, which didn't grow properly.

While John was dreaming of the circus I had the dubious privilege of living on its periphery. I spent a large part of my childhood working on the sideshows in seaside amusement parks in the evenings, at weekends and during the school holidays. Then I had to leave school at fourteen because I was needed in the family business, which meant, in the summer, working for twelve hours a day, seven days a week. To me, being a carney worker was anything but glamorous: it was heavy, rough and tiring and I bitterly resented being forced to do this rather than continue my education.

I had longed to stay on at school and learn, having daydreamed about the kind of boarding school to be found only in the pages of Angela Brazil and Enid Blyton wherein the naughty girls in the fourth form exchanged anxious confidences over Latin prep or during lacrosse practice and even if the geography teacher was a tartar the girls could indulge in midnight feasts in the dorm with the delicious food they all had stashed in the tuck boxes so lovingly supplied by our tragically absent parents. So my illusions about life were just as extreme as John's. In a way I yearned for the kind of life he was born to while he had pined for the colour and rawness of the life that was thrust upon me as the daughter of itinerant fairground workers.

When John was eight years old he was sent away to a prep school in Birchington – along with his tuck box, of course. When I was eight, war was declared and mother took us children to Oldham to live with our Lancashire grandparents. Father stayed behind to help guard Dover Harbour. My new school was an ugly soot-blackened building surrounded by high walls, where the cane was wielded often and with gusto by a sadistic old teacher who had been brought out of retirement to teach us to read, write and hate ourselves. John went on from Grenham House prep school to Sherborne, which he loathed, and where life was only just made bearable because he was good enough at cricket to get into the First Eleven.

He was bright enough to get by at Sherborne but had no academic ambitions and he hated the narrow-mindedness of a school that regarded a good pupil as one whose spirit had been broken in the name of conformity. He told me that the actor Robert Morley, who had suffered the same agonies at Wellington, when asked to return as a famous old boy to hand out the prizes, told the headmaster, 'Not without a sub-machine gun, and a fully armed platoon.' Perhaps it all just goes to show that whatever social class one comes from we all have our demons to fight.

Someone once said, 'Life is a shit sandwich: the more bread you have the less shit you have to eat,' but I don't agree that money and privilege make you less scared of life. As the poet Fran Landesman wrote, 'On our way to the stars, everybody gets scars.' However, it took me many years to understand this fully and stop feeling sorry for myself at times. I know now that I have been amazingly blessed and lucky.

John's father was a lawyer who rather assumed that his son would become one too. Although John knew by the time he left Sherborne that he wanted to become an actor, he was reluctant to express so daring, so improper an ambition and was articled to a respected firm of local solicitors. It soon became clear to John and to his employers that the majesty of the law was not going to be enriched by this young clerk's bungled or half-hearted efforts to uphold it and he eventually summoned up the courage to tell his parents that he danced to a different tune. John's father received the news with weary stoicism and just before his son's twenty-first birthday he gave his blessing to John's desire to become an actor.

John was given his train fare to London and an address in St John's Wood, where he found cheap lodgings and signed on at the Fay Compton Studio of Dramatic Art. Not quite RADA perhaps, but Miss Compton had a long and distinguished stage career behind her and her school was greatly respected. There were twenty-two girls and two male students, the other man being Alec Guinness. John said that it was obvious from the start that Alec would be a great actor, that he had the ability to inhabit the skin of whoever he portrayed, while John's characters were always marked with his particular leisurely and faintly ironic style. Typecasting set in early, I guess. Neither John nor Alec Guinness stayed at the school for more than a few months but they both picked up the rudiments of mime, film technique, fencing and tap dancing.

Apparently they had to polish their skills

with a number from *42nd Street* and were not very good, yet at the end of the term they both got engagements. John's first job was in repertory theatre in Edinburgh and Alec went into John Gielgud's *Hamlet* at the New Theatre in the West End of London and took the first steps in an acting career of celebrated brilliance. John never really got on with Shakespeare although he carried a few spears in various productions. Ibsen and Chekhov were more his style and later he liked the work of Harold Pinter to which he could bring those qualities of airiness and detachment for which he will always be remembered.

Whatever John was invited to do in various rep theatres all over Britain he did with a light heart, feeling blessed and lucky that he could make his living this way rather than in some worthy but stagnant office. He had found his métier and he was happy, never to my knowledge yearning for a greater stardom although as a young man he had the sort of good looks, manner and lovely voice that could have made a matinée idol of him if he had nursed such ambitions.

This is not to say that John was ever anything other than absolutely dedicated and professional. There were times when, in twice nightly rep, where two different plays were staged and two sets of lines had to be learned, he would sit up late into the night preparing uncomplainingly. He once said that he never lost the sense of happy wonder about doing the thing he loved and getting paid for it. It's a far cry from then to the present day when a young person can find instant fame in a soap opera, be a star for fifteen minutes and disappear without trace just as quickly.

I was with John once in a bar when a young woman came over and asked him how she could get into the business. She had done a bit of modelling, she said, and thought she might 'try her hand' at acting. John gently replied that you didn't 'try your hand' at acting: you either wanted to do it more than anything else and took every opportunity to work in any production, however humble and underpaid in order to learn your craft, or you simply wanted fame, which was a different thing entirely. All this was said, of course, with exquisite courtesy although he muttered a few sharper words to me as she wiggled away. He mourned the decline of the repertory theatre, which he believed was the best training for any aspiring actor. TV had already challenged the viability of most regional and provincial theatres as people stayed at home watching a small screen instead of sharing something alive and unique. How ironic that it was to be television which, latish in his life and career, brought him such fame, fond regard, recognition and security.

Throughout the thirties and up until the Second World War, which scattered or shattered so many lives, John worked at his craft. I was growing up in Ramsgate and Folkestone on the southerly Kent coast of Britain until the war sent my family away to live among the sooty satanic mills of Oldham in Lancashire, where the sun seldom seemed to make an appearance.

John's war was not too unpleasant, to be truthful. He turned up at his barracks on Salisbury Plain at roughly the right time but without his call-up papers. These had disappeared along with his Chelsea house, which was destroyed by a bomb some time in September 1940. Although he had been a public schoolboy and thus – ridiculously, perhaps – potentially 'officer material', John was obliged to complete basic squaddie training and never really had the wish or the will to issue orders and commands. Those barracks on Salisbury Plain saw the birth of

Sergeant Wilson: the well-educated, cultured, amused and laconic chap who simply thought that barking out pointless orders fell right into the 'life's too short' department. This was particularly so as John observed lesser but self-important men doing exactly that. He always had enough self-confidence and detachment to leave certain ambitions to others while amusing himself with quietly withering contempt if he saw them over-reach.

John was married by then to the very wealthy and glamorous June Melville whose father had built and managed several West End theatres, including the Shaftesbury where years later John appeared in the stage show of *Dad's Army*. June worked in theatre administration, and perhaps she was exasperated at times that her handsome husband seemed to have so few egotistical ambitions. They lived in a lovely house in Smith Street, Chelsea, which again had a grand piano in the pretty drawing-room and which housed his collection of gramophone records acquired over many years. When he arrived home one afternoon in September 1940 to find his home a bomb site it was the loss of those records that upset him most, not the loss of the other valuable possessions that had also gone up in smoke. Thus he joined the army carrying little but his golf clubs, which caused a certain amount of hilarity to the sergeant in charge of his troop.

In fact after the basic training period was over he said to John whom he called 'Lee Mesure' as he couldn't get his tongue round the name, 'When you turned up here it looked as if you thought you were coming on a long fucking weekend.' He also said that John would be bloody useless as a corporal let alone a sergeant, so he'd better try to become an officer. It was in a mood of euphoria on hearing this news that John stepped forward to volunteer for the parachute regiment whereupon the sergeant said out of the corner of his mouth, 'Don't be a cunt, Lee Mesure.'

Eventually, as John recalled, he ended up with one insecure pip on his shoulder and he often wondered how he got through the training, probably because like the Sergeant Wilson character he played in *Dad's Army* he was nice and kind to his men which made them want to be nice and kind to him. He did once drive a motorbike at a brick wall and just managed to fall off at the last moment. He never got on one again to my knowledge. He also made me laugh by telling me that part of his equipment when he first joined the army was a little sewing kit that was called a housewife – pronounced hussif, I think. He said he didn't open it once, but laid it out neatly on his bed during inspections. The thought of John attempting to thread a needle still makes me smile.

My war in Oldham was far less colourful, passing slowly in the frozen north of England. I remember trudging off to school in my clogs, dreading what fresh hell was waiting for me there. The classrooms had high windows so there was little scope for daydreaming or other creative thought and any lapse of attention would be halted by the swishing of the evil Miss Bridget's cane, so that the only sound to break the disciplined silence seemed to be the whimpering of her latest victim.

My father joined us in Lancashire to work in a munitions factory and, eventually, Grandma too consented to be driven from the companionable but limited comforts of the damp tunnels which served in Ramsgate as shelters. Originally enlarged from caves which had been used by smugglers many years before when the area survived on contraband, these tunnels had become home to local stalwarts who, clinging fiercely to their native ground, had turned into semi-troglodytes for the duration. Poor Grandma, how she hated Oldham: the dialect, the ugliness, the foreignness of it all. She epitomized the type of person who found purpose in wartime deprivations and the warm camaraderie that formed among neighbours who might otherwise have been prune-faced net curtain-twitching irritants. Anyway, she was an elderly woman and not minded to up sticks unless she had to.

While Mum was happy to be back at last among her own folk again, Grandma and I clung together for comfort, longing for the sweet-salt air of home and the wider skies of the south coast. However, we found a means of release and escape surprisingly close to home. Just found the corner was the Lyric cinema; in fact, the exit door was in the alley that ran along the bottom of our yard – directly opposite our outside privy. All very choice, as you can imagine, so it wasn't so odd that a generally grumpy old girl and a fretful young one would take comfort as often as we could in the miraculous, warm, heady darkness of the Lyric, where we enjoyed a glimpse of happier, more plentiful worlds. Grandma would take me twice a week (bi-weekly changes in the cinema double-bill programme was the thing in those days, like bi-weekly repertory theatre, so seeing four different films each week wasn't unusual). Other nights of the week I would either sneak into the fleapit if I could or on rare warm summer evenings when the projection room door was open I could be found on the privy roof listening to the sound track. I knew all the songs from the musicals of that era and great chunks of dialogue and as I had probably seen the film more than once already, I could visualize it all.

We ate reasonably well, I suppose, supplementing our rations when we could by recourse to the black-market economy which thrived everywhere in wartime, whatever others would have you believe. In every community there was a man who could find a nice piece of bacon, a few extra eggs or a pat of butter – at a price, of course. Those enormous humming, thrumming white refrigerators in the corner of every kitchen in American films and that cookie jar that was never empty came to exemplify for me a longing for that dazzling sense of plenty. My love of good food today relates, I'm sure, to the pinched wartime diet that we were officially constrained to endure most of the time.

When John's officer training was completed he was posted to India. One night on the way, in Port Said, he foolishly drank a whole bottle of Egyptian vodka and was very unwell until the boat reached Bombay when he perked up no end. He described the smells there as being a complete culture shock: a fusion of millions of curries, cooked over the centuries and mellowed to a faded spiciness. It certainly enhanced John's love of Indian food: he never tired of it – the hotter the better. I never quite got the hang of cooking Indian food at home – there never seemed to be a local shop with all the right herbs and spices in those days and the meat seemed to need a better marinade than I could muster. But we didn't have to resort to Vesta packets too often as there was usually a good local takeaway, even in our early days.

He finally disembarked at Poona from whence he was sent to Ahmadnagar for two years. He was given a bearer called Dohdiram who announced that he was also John's guardian angel and thus followed him everywhere, even when John wished that he wouldn't. John quickly tired of the conversation of the local residents, which was horribly charged with nostalgia for the great days of the Raj. He much preferred the company of the Sikhs, whose welfare and education were his responsibility.

At first, given the Sikh's warlike reputation, he was rather frightened of them but, with the help of Dohdiram, he came to admire and respect them. He was initially taken aback by their habit of sleeping in pairs, locked in each other's arms, and attempted on one occasion to separate two of them with his swagger stick. 'I wouldn't trouble yourself, if I was you, Sir,' advised his duty sergeant as he observed John's efforts to bring some British decency to the camp. 'They do it all the time and it don't affect them any.'

He spent his first leave in Bombay with Dohdiram in tireless attendance, in spite of John's entreaties that he should go and spend some time with his family. I'm sure that Dohdiram realized that being with John on leave in Bombay was far more exciting than staying at home. He and a fellow officer stayed at The Taj Mahal Hotel where they soon tired of the gentility of the place and the Gilbert and Sullivan selections offered by the band in the dining-room. They asked the waiter where the action took place in Bombay. 'Number four Grant Road,' was the reply. Years later John was on a quiz show; one of the questions was 'If good girls go to heaven, where do bad girls go?' 'Number four Grant Road' was John's speedy riposte, to which several men in the audience reacted with strangely raucous laughter.

During his service in India the war in Europe came to a close and John began to think of demob. Before leaving the army, however, he was sent to the North-West Frontier overlooking Afghanistan, to take charge of a troop of light tanks, patrolling the frontier – a most uncomfortable task as the region was very hot by day and freezing by night. Occasionally they were fired at by the Pathans but just by way of a bit of fun, and mostly in greeting, according to John.

However, his assignment was cut short when he got into a terrible muddle due to his poor map-reading skills. His downfall came when he got two tanks trapped up against the rocks and stuck in the under-growth. I can easily see John looking slightly flustered and mildly saying 'Oh Lor,' as he did when he inadvertently broke something. He wasn't exactly clumsy but he could find opening a letter or getting the cellophane off a packet of cigarettes troublesome. Eventually, help had to be sent for from HQ, the CO was not pleased and, in John's words, 'invited him to leave', proving that every cloud does have a silver lining.

On his way back from India he spent a week in a place called Deolali, which was so mind-numbingly boring that it popularized the expression 'Going Deolali', as in experiencing a sort of manic frustration. So far as I'm aware, John did not form any lasting army friendships in India. Poor man, I hope he wasn't too bored or lonely. John said that to save his sanity he kept a tight grip on the bar, thereby missing the all-male entertainment which was put on by a chap called Jimmy Perry. He saw what he had missed years later by watching dear Jimmy's TV series *It Ain't Half Hot Mum*. What a tangle of coincidence life is. Waved off by tearful Dohdiram and his large family, John left for home.

At about the same time that he was quietly jamming up the works on the Khyber Pass, my family had moved to the sinful city of

Blackpool which, although not far from Oldham, was very different. With the war drawing to a close, Dad was released from the aircraft factory and saw golden opportunities on the so-called Golden Mile, a tacky stretch of seafront chock-a-block with tawdry sideshows, arcades, funfairs and any number of diversions calculated to relieve jaded factory workers from nearby towns of their hard-earned and pathetically saved money.

Everything on offer was rubbish packed in cheap glitz. There was an ice-cream stall nearby which sold a sort of ghastly frozen custard (real cream was still a far-off luxury), and a pseudo-herbalist shop (full, no doubt, of quackery) on the corner of our street, which sold brightly coloured acidic drinks. One could guess which flavour was the most popular by the colourful pools of vomit leading from it. There was a stall selling hot pies that were warmed from beneath by buckets of hot water: heaven knows how many cases of food poisoning occurred in those days with few legal safety standards for foodstuffs and little understanding of such things. For a nation still forced to eat whale meat, sausages made from the parts of donkeys that you might choose not to contemplate, dodgy offal and other dubious delights, anything that looked good was popular.

I remember as a teenager longing for a box of chocolates more than anything in the world and dreaming of having a whole tin of peaches to myself. But it would be a long time before those dreams came true. I was by then about thirteen years old, had survived the ministrations of Miss Bridget and was enrolled in Tyldesley School, which was famous for its choir. There was an enormous gym with ropes, wall bars, vaulting horses, green fields in which to play hockey and games and – most important of all, the teachers were human beings – not a sadist among them. I fell in love with my English teacher who was amazed by my knowledge of the works of Charles Dickens. My northern grandfather, a superficially fierce and forbidding fellow and a staunch socialist of the old school, ex-mayor and alderman, had in his front parlour a huge bookcase filled with Dickens (his) and schoolgirls' annuals of the thirties (an aunt's), all of which I had devoured while sitting on an itchy horse-hair sofa there. Never being allowed the luxury of taking one away with me, I burrowed in that library as long as anyone would let me – or perhaps until they remembered that that was where I had vanished to.

Tyldesley School reinforced my love of learning, kindling the flames lit by madcap Bunty at Greystones, and Teresa of The Upper Third. However, on looking back on my life, I have had experiences that taught me more than I would ever have learned by sitting at a desk. So what if I never got to grips with the finer points of grammar. Can *you* tell me what a gerund is? I thought not. No one seemed to like me less for it although, as I mentioned earlier, I have always felt miserably conscious of my deplorable handwriting.

When John sailed away from Deolali and arrived home there was no one to meet him when his ship docked at Southampton since his ETA had been a bit vague. He went through the process of demobilization, swapping his becoming officer's uniform for a hideous brown demob suit, picked up £300 in back pay and such to get him started in Civvy Street and headed for Waterloo station in London. Before long it was clear that things at home had changed. His wife June and her family wanted him to continue working in the theatre under her direction but John had decided to seek a career in films. He was by then in his mid-thirties and wanted to make a bit more money than he had previously earned by touring in repertory theatre. He was also worried about being professionally tied to June, who had resorted to hitting the bottle in a big way during the war. It would not have been in John's nature to be censorious about this – after all, the poor woman had been left alone to run a notoriously 'sociable' business in his absence and her home had been blitzed. None the less, his tolerance was severely strained when she became hopelessly drunk in public, even, on one occasion – at a first night, no less – being asked to leave the theatre.

Apart from that, their war marriage, like many others, had been entered upon at a time of living dangerously – never knowing what the next air raid would bring. Now that peace had arrived there was less excitement in a drab post-war world and their former passion became as flat as stale champagne. John moved out, took a bachelor flat and then set about knocking on film agents' doors in Wardour Street. Few even creaked open. Discouraged yet undeterred by his failure to break into films, he went back to work at Croydon rep. At least he was working and keeping his head above water.

Dear John

Thank you for your letter. I tried to have a word with you the other night but as always you were surrounded by people.

We have very much enjoyed having you with us and I am bitterly sorry to be losing you now. Had I known that you wanted a change I could have offered you something by the sea but I suppose that the die is irrevocably cast by now. If at any time you would like to return, do let us know and I can assure you that no one will be more delighted to have you back again than

Yours sincerely

JB

This period at Croydon rep was a particularly enjoyable one and ever afterwards he retained an affection for the drab little suburb – blessed though it was in those days with a society aerodrome – and its repertory theatre. When he had left he received the letter from the management which he kept and treasured – the first confirmation that he was valued as an actor.

Most actors find it impossible to go home to bed right after a performance. The adrenalin is still flowing and as theatre actors can sleep late they usually seek out places where they can mingle with their fellow thespians. One popular venue in those days was the Players' Theatre in Villiers Street, just off the Strand, an old-fashioned music hall where most aspiring actors of the day trod the famous boards at one time or another. The restaurant there was presided over by Bruce Copp who was later to open many successful restaurants in the sixties and seventies, one being the restaurant of the Mermaid Theatre opened by Bernard Miles, another the Hungry Horse in Chelsea and later the famous Establishment club. Bruce was a close friend of Hattie Jacques. She was a big star at the Players' and was later to become more widely celebrated in comedy roles on radio and in television and films.

John was immediately dazzled by her talent, her personality and her beauty; before long they were deeply in love. The centre of a large circle of friends, Hattie had wit and a sense of fun; she was also practical, motherly and a great hostess. Later in her career Hattie was to allow herself to be typecast, even caricatured, as obese battleaxes, so younger readers may find it hard to visualize the exotic, Juno-esque and sensual figure she cut at the time. She rather resembled Maria Callas, having the same colouring and flashing vivacity.

Divorce was a sluggish business in Britain in those days, even when it was by mutual consent. So while those legal wheels ground on John moved in with Hattie who lived in a big Victorian house in Eardley Crescent, Earls Court, in west London. Bruce Copp rented the basement, an actress friend had a bed-sit in the attic and Hattie presided over it all like an endlessly warm and welcoming mother hen. John loved her eccentricities and her talent. She was already making a mark for herself beyond the clubby environ-ment of the Players' and her big break had come when she joined ITMA in 1946 as Sophie Tuckshop, a precocious schoolgirl with a big appetite and who was always being sick. ITMA, of course (once again for the education of my younger readers) was the hugely successful BBC radio series *It's That Man Again*.

At that time, Hattie almost celebrated her

size, carrying it well and dressing up to it in swirling cloaks and wraps borrowed from the Players' wardrobe department. She was also very graceful. I remember her at the Players' singing a song called 'I Don't Want to Play in Your Yard' with the very young Clive Dunn who also made regular appearances there. Hattie floated about the stage so smoothly that she appeared to have wheels under her long skirts. John was swept into her life and overwhelmed. The house at Eardley Crescent was a meeting place for talent, with Hattie's friends popping in all the time. One of these was Tony Hancock, another Players' regular, and he and John became firm friends.

Meanwhile, during those post-war years when victory was supposedly ours but a grim and stingy regime of rationing and deprivation prevailed, I was growing up quickly. My first experience of grief came with the death of my grandmother, a victim of pneumonia at the age of sixty-four. She had stayed in Oldham with Grandpa when we moved to Blackpool and though she visited us there from time to time, she was longing for the day when we would all return to Ramsgate. Sadly it never came for her. Her homesick soul, unable to wait any longer, had gone on ahead, back to the coast of Kent. I was inconsolable. That there was no Grandma in the world just wasn't possible: she had been my best friend and my rock. Her love for me was my only true certainty, her company a never wavering joy. She was a big dark-haired woman of Romany descent (something seldom discussed in the family) and like Hattie she was warm hearted and light on her feet. She and Mum had never really got on, mother being a practical north country woman and Grandma an emotionally generous peasant, giving time and hospitality to anyone who had a touching story.

Grandma was the one who had made Christmas joyful, for instance. Hoarding and saving her pennies and subscribing to those Christmas Clubs whereby working people of the time were able to accumulate credit at local shops, she bought and stored dried fruits and sweets months before the day. Drawers and cupboards were full of delicious rustling secrets and during the week leading up to Christmas her big kitchen table was her work place. I would sit at one end making paper chains while she, at the other, would be rolling pastry for the sausage rolls and mince tarts, boiling a huge ham, making the stuffing for the turkey, while we sang carols together. All the food was stored in the pantry, or cold room, at the back of the kitchen in those pre-refrigerator days. Grandpa would go down the pub and bring back a jug of beer for Grandma, lemonade for me and it seemed to me that I was the richest, happiest girl in the whole world. When she was gone she took the magic with her.

In later years, when much water and some blood had flowed under the bridge and I met Hattie Jacques and grew so fond of her, it was she who reminded me of much of the magic of Christmas as she prepared for it in an undaunted spirit of plenty and generosity despite Britain's post-war restrictions. Like Grandma, Hattie began planning for it around September, making lists and checking who would be able to join the crowd around her table. Her Christmases were often three-day affairs in which every meal was planned in advance with choices of starters and puddings. Of course Hattie's Christmases were more sumptuous than Grandma's. We lived in different worlds, but the feelings they evoked were the same. Once, on a Christmas Eve in Hattie's kitchen where I was helping to prepare vegetables and such like for the coming festivities I had a strong feeling that Grandma was there looking in on us and sharing the fun.

When my dad took Grandma's tired old body back to Ramsgate for the burial and saw the old town dusting itself down, he found Grandma's house still intact, so he sent for the rest of us. VJ day came soon afterwards and final peace was declared. Mum and Dad set to the task of cleaning up the house and making it habitable and for the first time in my life I was given a room of my own. I joined the local library and the youth club, and enrolled for evening classes but, alas, a scholar's life was not to be. Dad was setting up a few deals at Merrie England, a local fun-fair, for a bingo stall and a rifle range and I was included in his plans so any hope of further education was scuppered. I can't say I was at all happy about this but I didn't have the guts to resist. I'd been brought up to be obedient and had possibly scented some disapproval from my parents about aspirations which would distance me from them. At any rate, I put up and shut up. The following Easter Merrie England opened up its doors, we were back in business and it was goodbye to evening classes and the hope of any sort of escape via education and back to the carney world.

At about the same time John was making a film called *Escape from Broadmoor*, his first, which he described as being hilarious for all the wrong reasons. The leading lady, whom he described as a shy retiring girl, acted throughout as if in a trance and when John had to knock the villain on the head with the butt of a revolver he knocked the poor man unconscious, although he said it was the lightest of taps – on screen it certainly looked as if he was swatting flies. This and other potboilers were all that came his way during those years but whenever he spoke to me of this period it was with affectionate nostalgia and I never gained the impression that he was unhappy or frustrated at the time. He was, as he often said, just a jobbing actor and happy to be in work. I suppose he must have lacked ambition but the drive towards fame and success is not always attractive in a human and John's lazy charm brought him just about as much work as he could be bothered with. He was in several of the Edgar Lustgarten shorts, and, in contrast, a couple of slapstick Old Mother Riley films where he was on the receiving end of several custard pies. He accomplished all such work with quiet professionalism, happier to drink and smoke with his friends after a show or a day's filming than to 'schmooze' with the casting agents. He enjoyed a drink and a smoke until he died and regarded these as innocent pleasures and no one's business but his own if he got a finger-wagging about the perils of alcohol and cigarettes.

Hattie, meanwhile, was doing rather better: she won the part of a tough shop-floor welder in a Bernard Miles film called *Chance of a Lifetime*, made easier for her as she had for a time been a welder in a factory during the war. She had also been a nurse during the blitz, which must have been handy in the Carry On era when she often played the fierce, turkey-bosomed hospital matron. But even though her star was rising and John was still on the periphery of fame, Hattie made sure that he never felt over-shadowed by her growing popularity. She always encouraged and cared for him and believed in his talent.

I suppose he was rather passive about things. The house at Eardley Crescent was comfortable and welcoming to return to after fruitlessly and perhaps not very aggressively knocking on doors in Wardour Street in Soho, the hub of the British film world. It must have been nice for him to feel cherished and looked after, just accepted for himself. Hattie's cooking was legendary, guided by Bruce Copp's flair for making a banquet out of a pinch of this, a scrap of that and whatever else was available and affordable. The two of them created gastronomic miracles.

Quite how Hattie found all those wonderful foodstuffs remains a mystery – perhaps she knew a Private Walker type and had access to the black economy that provided many Britons with a little extra in those days. Anyway, as Elizabeth David rather tartly pointed out in her classic book about Mediterranean food, published very early in the 1950s, even then most of the ingredients demanded by her recipes could be sought out in Britain if you actually cared about what you ate and citing shortages was little more than an excuse for the lazy, indifferent or mean. So by the early 1960s there was absolutely no reason to be stingy or un-imaginative in the kitchen. John was contented and the household ran smoothly thanks to Hattie and Bruce's organizing gifts. There were dinner parties with friends on the same rungs of the theatre ladder, Clive Dunn, Tony Hancock, Joan Sims, Frankie Howerd and Beryl Reid – all to become great stars in due course. They were all of an age and, freed from the shackles of a war which had stifled their budding talents, they were now beginning to regain a foothold in the world they had missed so much.

One day, after John and Hattie had been living together for around five years he received a gracious telegram from June Melville saying, 'The cage is open, darling, you can fly away now'. The divorce had at last been finalized. Hattie proposed: dear John would never have bothered to get around to it after the failure of his marriage to June, but Hattie was determined so they were married at Kensington register office in April 1952 and soon had two fine sons, Robin, born on 22 March 1953 and Kim on 12 October 1956. It was about this same time, 1955, that John's professional life received a significant boost when he received a phone call from an old friend who had written a script for a film called *Josephine and Men*, to be directed by Roy Boulting and produced by John, his twin brother. Apparently Roy would like to meet him, meaning, I'm sure, that the writer had had a word with Roy and there was a part for John. Of course he jumped at the offer of a part in a film which had a cast headed by Jack Buchanan and with supporting actors Peter Finch and Glynis Johns. It was the beginning of his relationship with the Boultings who were to direct and produce a string of English films at Shepperton Studios that are still regarded as classics of that particular genre and in which John's cameo performances are legendary. It was mainly light comedy, but always with the cutting edge of social observation – usually slightly darker than those other brilliant films being made at Ealing Studios at roughly the same time.

The second film was *Private's Progress*, which brought his first encouraging mention in a national newspaper by a young critic called Dilys Powell who continued to give him good notices throughout his career. On one occasion she gave a luke-warm review of a British film saying that it would have been enhanced by the presence of John Le Mesurier. Miss Powell became the doyenne of British film critics, reviewing for the *Sunday Times* until her death over forty years later. Her judgements were sometimes harsh but always astute and she was a champion talent-spotter. John appeared in several of the Boultings' films, *Baby and the Battleship* in 1956, *Brothers in Law* in 1957, *I'm All Right Jack* in 1959 and *School for Scoundrels* in 1960. He became a member of the repertory troop of support actors. Now he was working constantly and was always grateful to the Boultings. He said that they were demanding and difficult at times and after a day's work he and his fellow thesps really felt they had earned their money – even though it wasn't very much. He later told me that he never really believed that he deserved his fame but realized that he owed a lot to his air of bewildered innocence – a decent chap all at sea in a chaotic world not of his own making. True, perhaps, but it was the essential honesty of such performances which made people love him.

John's lucky star was still shining when he met Freddie Joachim who was to become his agent until he retired fifteen years later. Freddie was respected in the business and had on his books about twelve actors, including Dirk Bogarde. He refused to represent women on the grounds that they were more complicated than men in their private lives. I don't think I would have got on with him but I didn't have to worry about that as I never met him. Even John only saw Freddie once a year for lunch but he was canny and astute where John was concerned. 'Always keep yourself a little bit rare, John' was his sound advice and even though John could have earned more in other stables that's what he did. Little by little John was becoming a National Treasure...

In Ramsgate I was growing up fast, still stuck on the fairground in the summers, where I was as good a grafter as any of the old barkers who came down from London every season. I looked so trustworthy and innocent that I could have sold pigswill to the farmers. If there was trouble among the drunken day-trippers Dad would send me out to calm things down, believing that drunks never hit women. He was right up to a point because I could always disarm them with my dirndl-skirted charms.

When I was eighteen a friend who was walking out with a carney worker from Margate just along the coast, fixed me up on a blind date with his friend, another seasonal grafter who worked as a walkie snap-photographer in Dreamland Park. You paid your shilling and hoped to God the fellow would have the decency to send the family snapshot on later. Few people had their own cameras in those days. I fell in love on sight. He was tall and dark with green eyes and charm in buckets and spades. He was also amazingly well read and could quote poetry by the hour if I let him. I discovered later that he had been stricken with tuberculosis in his late teens and had spent eighteen months in a sanatorium where he had met an English teacher who had taught him to use his time there learning the joys of literature. By the time he left he was in charge of the hospital library. He was custom-made for me – on our second date the following night he tried to seduce me under a tree while quoting from Andrew Marvell's 'To his Coy Mistress'. He tried again on the third date but my passion for him was tempered by the fear of what my father would do should I get into trouble, as the euphemism for falling pregnant went in those days. So I stayed coy and 'Into the ashes went his lust'. On the fourth date he stood me up and broke my heart.

His name was Douglas Malin and never in

the following four years did I forget him. I was twenty-two when I met him again in Dreamland and he looked even more gorgeous than ever. This time I stopped being coy and we were married two months later on 22 October 1953.

By this time Dad had given up the fairground to my great relief and I was working as a dental nurse in Broadstairs, three miles along the coast. Douglas worked in Dreamland every summer and in the winter took whatever work was going in order to make ends meet. We rented a modest flat and though we lacked money we had lots in common and were never bored, thanks largely to Doug's clever mind and his love of books. Lacking the luxury of even a radio in those days, we resorted to the public library for our entertainment. At night we would sit by the fire reading aloud to each other. Sorry if I'm making all this seem too, too, desperately romantic... Because of Doug's startlingly good looks the local dramatic society lured him into taking the lead in Christopher Fry's *The Lady's Not for Burning*. He was exceptionally good in it and I was prompt, being heavy with child at the time and loaded also with pride. I learned the entire play and could prompt without a script. To this day I can quote huge passages from it.

On 10 June 1957 our son, David Mark, was born, a beautiful carbon copy of his handsome dad. But while my life was now fulfilled, with Douglas it was quite the opposite. Becoming a father meant becoming somebody with adult responsibilities and now he had to stop being Peter Pan and help me to take care of the new life.

By the autumn of that year Doug knew that he wanted to act professionally. His sister Kathy was in drama school at Rose Bruford College and from her he picked up tips on acting, make-up, names of teachers and the surprisingly complex matter of how to walk across a stage. Armed with this meagre knowledge and grafter's bluff, he went off to London and did the rounds of the agents' offices. It wasn't long before the potential of his looks and charm were recognized. He found an agent who made him change his name to Mark Eden, saying that Douglas Malin was too ordinary. He did a TV commercial or two then bluffed his way into Swansea rep where he seriously began to learn his trade.

Those were lean years, the hardest I had ever endured. I could no longer work full-time with a child to look after and Mark's unreliable pittances were barely enough to keep the three of us in bread and jam. Thank God for my parents who looked after David during the summer months while I worked part-time in the box-office of the Pavilion Theatre by the harbour. It was my first encounter with the professional theatrical people and I was fascinated by them. The star of the show was Reg Dixon, a comedian, and he and his wife were very kind to me, as were the rest of the cast. We all became friends and they urged me to go to London and get a full-time job, put David in a nursery school, and be near my husband. Their advice was sound but belated as by the autumn of 1959 Mark had met an actress in Nottingham rep and had fallen in love.

Our marriage was over but not the friendship which remains strong to this day. Mark has always felt guilty about the end of our marriage but it was the watershed that was eventually to lead me to John. I dare say I wailed and howled at the time, but looking back I can't regret anything about that first marriage.

In London John and Hattie were becoming

household names. Hattie had teamed up with Eric Sykes, which led to a popular TV sitcom wherein they played an exasperated but ever-loving brother and sister. Radio stardom came when she took over the only female role in *Hancock's Half Hour*. There were many Carry On films as well, with their steady stable of much-loved comic actors like Sid James, Barbara Windsor, Joan Sims and Kenneth Williams.

By the time Hattie gave birth to their second son, Kim, in 1956, Eardley Crescent was an even more hectic hive of activity. There were various au pair girls over the years and even a secretary to keep their affairs in order, as well as a cleaner. Both John and Hattie (always 'Jo' to John – because her real name was Josephine), later regretted how little time they saw of their sons when they were small and found that along with success the carefree days had flown.

Hattie, in addition to her acting career, was deeply involved in charity work, particularly on behalf of sick or handi-capped children. John always believed that she needed to be liked and respected for herself, something she felt did not come easily in her professional life. She was a comedy star, yes, but always the Aunt Sally, the faintly ludicrous figure of authority to be knocked over by other people's jokes. As a charity worker she was seen in an entirely different light. By expressing her loving and caring personality in this way, Hattie found the strength and energy she needed. Being a great organizer she was always setting up schemes to raise money: there were art exhibitions with contributions by celebrities, variety concerts, dances, and if that wasn't enough she would take out short leases on empty premises and run charity shops, such as the one in King Street, Hammersmith, where she sold second-hand clothes for the Leukaemia Foundation.

Eventually her charity foundation appointed a driver to get her about: a good-looking, amusing charmer called John Scofield, he had recently lost his son to leukaemia and this had led to the break-up of his marriage. Who better to turn to for sympathy than the great-hearted Hattie who took him under her wing as she always did with those who needed her. He was a very handsome man with lots of charm and gave Hattie the undivided attention and support that John, working away from home so frequently, was unable to do. All this was a very novel experience to Hattie, who was used to being the mother figure with John. Scofield, on the other hand, was earthy, sexy and rough and made her feel like a young girl again. He became a fixture at Eardley Crescent, soon under the sheets, as well as Hattie's wing. At first John didn't seem to be aware of what went on during his absences: after all there were always people coming and going and staying over in spare rooms or on sofas, and John was often either working long hours or away on location. By the time John chose to notice the regularity of Scofield's presence, he had ingratiated himself with Robin and Kim as well and Hattie had already lost her heart.

As I was later to learn and see for myself, jealousy was not an emotion that John cared to admit to, let alone display openly. He simply hoped that the infatuation would run its course. Everybody loved Hattie and she wanted to be needed, so he kept his head down and carried on as best he could. However, it became impossible to ignore the situation when Scofield began to show undue familiarity and even possessive aggression at John's presence, like a young lion daring to challenge the older one. John's gentle nature could not deal with that sort of behaviour. He withdrew more and became deeply unhappy: his comfortable marriage was in jeopardy and he had no weapons with which to fight for his wife and his children. He opted to go away for a while after a showdown in which Hattie openly, and in Schofield's presence, declared her love for his rival. When he returned he found that Scofield had moved into his home and his bed, and he and his things had been relegated to a bed-sitting room.

By the spring of 1960 I had gathered my courage and moved to London, leaving David with my parents during the week and rushing home every weekend and at holidays to be with him. I worked as a dental nurse at a practice in Drury Lane and shared a flat with friends, two gay dancers I had met during a summer season in Ramsgate. One of them was Lindsay Kemp who went on to become the most distinguished British mime artiste of his time and a profound influence, some years later, on David Bowie. My increased London earnings enabled me to provide lots of hitherto unknown treats for my son, but I was racked with guilt about leaving him and always felt I should give him more. My friend Sheila fixed me up with a second job, working in the evenings at the bar of the Queen's Theatre in Shaftesbury Avenue. I absolutely loved this work, being outgoing and – at the time – full of youthfully innocent flirtatiousness. It felt in some ways like an extension of my carney work, but in a slightly more sophisticated ambience. I was popular and earned good tips, and although my days were busy I could now support my son properly and give him extra presents and luxuries as well as the things he needed without putting a strain on Mark, who was still struggling to get ahead and learn his craft as an actor.

After my stint in the bar at the Queen's Theatre, I would usually meet my friend Sheila, another workaholic who worked as a shipping clerk by day and at the Aldwych Theatre by night, and we would go for a drink in a Soho club called the Fifty. The owners were old friends of hers and it was somewhere we could meet and unwind on our way home. Sheila lived with her mother in St Martin's Lane, just up from Trafalgar Square and I was in Lansdowne Crescent in Holland Park. Looking back it seems extraordinary to me that two humble working girls could have afforded to stay in what are now some of London's smartest areas. Things change: Notting Hill was considered the social pits at the time. The clientele at the Fifty was a mixture of theatrical and gay and one of the regulars was a choreographer and dancer named John Heawood. He had recently choreographed *The Boyfriend* (much later to be filmed by Ken Russell, starring Twiggy), which had had its debut at the Players' Theatre before going into the West End proper. He also created all the dancing in the London stage production of *Irma La Douce* which had been a big hit on both sides of the Atlantic. Shirley Maclaine starred in the film a few years later.

John Heawood was a friend of Hattie, John and Bruce Copp who was by now managing the Establishment Club in Greek Street, where Lenny Bruce made his celebrated, or some would say disastrous, London debut – it depended on how broadminded you were. Bruce had been vilified in his native New York and his humour was just as controversial in London, based as it was on his heroin addiction and his fearless, then shocking references to racial prejudices and sexual taboos.

The Establishment was an entirely new concept in entertainment and it has never been surpassed. For a start its cabaret was fronted by the *Beyond the Fringe* team of Dudley Moore, Peter Cook, Alan Bennett and Jonathan Miller after they had made such a success of their Cambridge Footlights show at the Edinburgh Festival. They appeared nightly in the cellar bar and on the ground floor was another bar leading to the cabaret room. Every fashionable star of the day appeared there: Frankie Howerd made a famous comeback there, Libby Morris, Peter Cook and Annie Ross all made legendary appearances and the place was awash with rich and famous punters. Even before it opened its doors the Establishment had a waiting list of 5000, and if you weren't a member there there was no way you could get in. It's hard to explain now how important and influential satire was in Britain at the time – we're all so used to irreverence and sharp political jabs and stabs from our comics now. It all seemed very new and daring at those little clubs forty years ago…

The box-office was presided over by George Erskine Jones, another choreographer and dancer who had danced with and learned his craft from Kathleen Dunham in America. George was wicked, witty and could be vitriolic should someone try to push his way into the club uninvited. On one occasion a minor member of the royal family assumed with a combination of arrogance and desperate cool, that he could enter on the strength of his name and was sent huffing and puffing off the premises by the unimpressed dragon of the gates.

One night Sheila and I were having a much needed after-work drink at the Fifty with John Heawood when he invited us to join him at *the* Establishment. We were both astounded. 'Do you mean *the* Establishment?' gasped Sheila. 'Nobody can get in there unless they're famous.' 'Nonsense, dear,' said Heawood, 'I'm a friend of the guy who runs it.'

That night my life changed for ever. We were ushered into the club like two VIPs instead of a couple of theatre barmaids and were introduced to George Erskine Jones and Bruce Copp who, thirty-six years on, I count as one of my closes friends. As I stood by the bar clutching my drink, my head on a swivel as I recognized familiar faces among the crowd, John Heawood asked Bruce if there were 'any chums in tonight, dear?' 'John Le Mesurier's watching the show but he'll be out any minute now,' replied Bruce and left us to attend to business. 'Who's John Le Mesurier?' I asked. 'You'll know his face when you meet him,' said Heawood. And indeed I did as soon as he came ambling towards us.

We were introduced and for the first time I looked into the kind brown eyes of the man who for the next twenty-one years was to bring to my life a great fund of experience and a deep and abiding love – and upon whom I was to inflict considerable pain.

2

It is only clear in retrospect, as is so often the case with momentous events, that that night in 1962 was a watershed in both our lives. To me at the time he was a polite, almost elderly gentleman (he was fifty to my thirty-one) who in spite of his air of melancholy seemed to have a wonderfully rueful sense of humour. I was slightly in awe of him, not having encountered many celebrities unless I served them from behind a bar, but by the end of that evening I was completely at ease in his company.

We had all removed to the basement bar to hear the Dudley Moore Trio. Before the set Dudley came over to speak to John, whom he knew well. At one point Dudley asked if I had a favourite song and when I told him that I loved a number called 'What's New?' John raised his eyebrows. 'How on earth does a slip of a girl like you know an old song like that?' he exclaimed, adding, 'It happens to be my favourite song too.'

I said that I loved the old torch songs and

ballads and could reel off any number of lyrics, just as I had memorized poetry when I was younger. John was mad about modern jazz but liked most music and often said he was frustrated musician himself. 'Perhaps when someone special is playing at Ronnie Scott's you'd like to come along with me, my little friend?' That meeting might not have seemed much on which to base a lifetime's relationship but a tenuous bond was formed right away. In the argot of the time, we were on the same wavelength. By the end of the evening when we thanked Bruce for his hospitality he told Sheila and me that any time we cared to return we had only to ask for him at the door. John then drove us home and deposited us in gentlemanly fashion at our respective doors. In the course of one evening I had made three new friends and my life was heading in a new direction.

Our courtship progressed so gradually it would be hard to say when friendship began to give way to something deeper. John would take me out to dinner about once a week and I began to look forward to these dates with increasing pleasure. Theatre barmaids in my day would be cashed up, cleaned up and out of the theatre before the last bum had returned to its seat after the interval, so it would still be reasonably early when John met me outside or in a nearby pub. We would dine in Soho, sometimes going on to the Establishment or Ronnie Scott's to hear some jazz. It was good to be able to share in the glow of affection that people had for John: waiters, musicians and fellow actors all treated me with deference and respect because I was his friend and that feeling endures to this day. Whenever someone connects my name with John people display a little extra warmth towards me. His sons have found the same.

It was some time before John began to talk to me about his life at Eardley Crescent and his misery there. Of course I knew that he was married to Hattie Jacques and that by then things were going badly but, in general, the problem was not discussed outside her circle of loyal friends, which included Bruce Copp and John Heawood. I knew John well enough by now to wait until he was ready to tell me himself and when he did, I offered no opinions or advice but simply listened. I knew that what John most wanted then was for John Scofield to leave and for things to revert back to normal. John loved Hattie: as yet I was just his friend and confidante.

Because there was no sexual tension between us I could be as honest about my private life as he was and could talk to him about admirers and other dates as if he was an older brother.

When Hattie heard about me from John I was invited to a party at Eardley Crescent. Looking back I realize that a spot of matchmaking was going on – nothing could have suited Hattie more than for John to find someone too to ease her guilt. But things had not yet reached that stage between us, nor would they for quite some time. However, even though I had already formed a few private opinions about the situation, when I met Hattie I really took to her. Her big heart and generosity of spirit were impossible to resist and I became one of the many who felt at ease, indeed welcomed and cherished, in her large and untidy house. She exuded kindness and received devoted affection from others in return.

Of course John loved her, as did her new man in his way, although he would one day break her heart so completely that it never mended. I could see at once how she drew such depths of loyalty from her friends. Like a little girl, I wanted to move immediately into the warmth and abundance of her beautiful, cosy home, to be cared for under her earth-motherly wing. Hattie was splendidly emblematic of the fact that love does not have to be rationed, that giving to one does not necessarily mean depriving another: she always had enough for everyone. But being loved and being in love are different matters and there was only room in her heart for this one new romantic attachment. She couldn't hide how mad about Scofield she was. In complete contrast to John, Scofield was a good-looking cockney with a macho charm that made Hattie feel like a young and giddy girl and, at the beginning, he seemed to need her as much as she wanted him. I did not know what to make of him: part of me was drawn to his likeable manner but another part wondered if he was little more than a chancer exploiting Hattie's largesse. While another part was beginning to wonder where, if anywhere, I fitted into all this and I certainly hated to see John so sad and humiliated. But Hattie was in love, common sense had evaporated as happens when one attains that glorious and ghastly state and John hadn't got a hope.

So as the weeks and months went by John

and I became a habit although at times his melancholy was catching. Often during our evenings together he would arrive in tears or break down later; I could usually cheer him up temporarily but his situation was at stalemate. One evening when he and Sheila came round to my flat for dinner he was in a particularly bad way over the situation at home and, try as I might, I had not been able to cheer him up. Finally, I became exasperated with him, pleaded a headache and went off to bed. He immediately wrote me a contrite note:

Eardley Crescent
Tuesday

I have just come in darling, I hope you are sleeping as I write this or at least having an early night. I think it was about 11.40 when I left, I rang Sheila just now who was up and bright and sprightly and in the kitchen. I said I was sorry if I had made her conscious of my stupidity – 'I hadn't' she exclaimed so that was that and I put the phone down.

I know you were tired this evening, if you can, please forgive me for being tiresome and boring. I love you somewhat and would like to go on seeing you. I care for your friendship and all the fun we have together; but please be honest with me and tell me if you don't want to know any more because of my situation. I will make one good clean exit and go for ever. I am a little distraught as I write this but it is the truth.

Your loving friend

John

By the spring of 1963 I was missing my son badly and tired of my job in Drury Lane where the dentist I worked for was a smug little creep with a bad chair-side manner. One morning he bullied a child and I spoke up against him, telling the boy's parents in the waiting-room to take the child to a decent dentist. Then, with a light heart, I collected my things and walked out. Happily I had just been paid as it was Friday and this prompted me to go home for the summer. I had managed to save some money by having two jobs but both playing and working hard had left me exhausted and I was ready for a break. Dad by then had opened a large self-service seafood cafeteria on Ramsgate front and also rented a cockle-and-whelk stall at

Ramsgate dog-track three evenings a week, which he wanted me to run.

I enjoyed working at the dogs. Weather permitting, it was out in the fresh air and at weekends I could take David with me as he did not have to get up for school the next morning. It was quite a change from the sophistication of the life I had in London, but the pleasure of being with my son more than compensated.

Sheila, who used to spend her summer holidays in Ramsgate as a child, often came down to see me at weekends. She loved the atmosphere at the dog-track and was quite a gambler. While I sold my old-fashioned sea-food delights she would bring me drinks and place bets. She gave me two tips: during the parade and before betting, if a dog has a hard-on or takes a crap, put your money on it. It always seemed to work.

By coincidence, John and Hattie had a house nearby in Margate. Hattie's mother, Mary, lived there and it was a base for the children during their summer holidays. Occasionally John would come over to visit me, bringing his younger son Kim to play with David who was the same age. Once or twice he drove me to the dog-track, carrying my stock in the boot of his car, and would stand by the stall signing autographs while I worked. I would send him off to place a bet should a dog take a dump during the grand parade. It was a strange courtship.

Being with John had become as comfortable as wearing a pair of old slippers. He sent me postcards when he was on location and would occasionally phone me for a pep talk when he was feeling low. Two of his letters from late in 1963 indicate the kind of pressure he was under.

Eardley Crescent
Thursday

I thought I would send a letter to you, darling, at Ramsgate, can't say today went with a swing. Had difficulties with Tania Levine at rehearsal in that cold, damp ill heated room. Must take my overcoat and thick socks I suppose.

I thought about you a lot and I was sorely tempted to just say 'Hullo' on the phone that wretched instrument though can be hopelessly inadequate at times and tones of voice etc can get misconstrued. Whatever happens I cannot lose you entirely, you mean more to me than *anyone*.

I am going to try and get things sorted out so that I will be a better person for you and others.

Everything is pressing in on me at the moment and I am going to try and rid myself of some other unnecessary entanglements. If you need me for anything during the day, *whatever* it is, worry or anxiety or just loneliness, you will get me on CUN 8210 from 10.30 all the coming week till 5 up until Oct 27th.

Please send me a note very soon just to say how you are.

God bless you.

John xx

Eardley Crescent
Tuesday evening

Darling Joan

It is only 9.30 and I am in my room. Another worrying day at rehearsal, I have said my lot about it and am trying very hard not to hit or shout at Tania for being such a berkette.

It finished me at the end of the day when

the author, after a particularly horrific run through, came to me and said 'Thank You John, you were always my favourite actor, you were so astringent and witty.' I did not know where to look and simply muttered something like 'Thank you' under my breath.

I look forward to seeing you. I have a suit on and a tie! They were all quite astonished when I arrived at rehearsal this morning. They asked me why I was dressed as I was, and I said that I was going to do something nice! This is aimed at being a lighthearted note.

I look forward to seeing you, I might well love you.

John xx

While spending most of that year in Ramsgate, I returned a few times to London to stay with Sheila and always went to the Establishment with her and John to see Bruce and Heawood. During one of these weekends Bruce offered me the use of his flat in St George's Square, Pimlico, as he was moving into a new house. Heawood was looking for a central place to live and Bruce suggested we share the flat as long as I took responsibility for the tenancy. He also offered me a job at the Establishment, serving drinks in the downstairs bar. The hours were long from 11.00 at night till 3.00 in the morning but the money was good.

And so that winter when the dog-track closed, I regretfully left David with my parents, having arranged with Bruce to take alternate Saturdays off so that I could have both long and short weekends in Ramsgate, and I moved back to London. Needing the money and not wanting to do nothing all day until it was time to start my shift at night, I took a day job at Gibbs Pepsodent in Portman Square (where I was nominally in charge of the complaints department), and settled myself and Heawood into our new billet. Johnny was a wonderful flatmate. He was domestically hopeless, which is why Bruce had put me in charge of things, but he made me laugh and he taught me a lot about life.

The winter of 1963 was one of the happiest times I have ever known. It was this happiness which enabled me to cram so much activity into my days. I was surrounded by interesting and stimulating people and I floated through my work held aloft by some divine energy. I would get up at 7.30, leave for the toothpaste company office at 8.30 and work until 5.00, when I would be met by John who would take me for a drink or an early dinner. Then back to my flat to change quickly and prepare for work at the Establishment. If I didn't have a date I would go home and rest for a few hours before the night's work. I call it work, and indeed it was demanding, but it was rather like going to a party every night. Every well-known face in the business would visit the Establishment, legendary musicians from Duke Ellington and Count Basie's bands would come to sit in with the Dudley Moore Trio and big names in the theatre came there after work to unwind.

That winter was also particularly cold and every weekend I went to Ramsgate. I would wake bleary and leave London around lunchtime on Saturdays and return on Sunday evening. This was such a short time with David that I made a supreme effort to go straight from work on those alternate Fridays, whatever the hour. On the long weekends, I would catch the 4.30 a.m. paper train from London Bridge. Before leaving the club at 3.30 I would make myself a sandwich and fill a hot-water bottle and settle myself in a first-class compartment to sleep with the bottle clasped to me. I was befriended by the guard who always gave me a cup of tea from his thermos with the morning paper and kept an eye on me as I slept with my head on a cushion from his van. When I arrived at Ramsgate a local newsagent, who was waiting for the papers, would give me a lift home, so I had quite a nice little system going. Home at last, I would let myself in and crawl into bed beside the warm, sleepy body of my son. Weekends were for David alone, but it was playtime for us both, and our Sunday evening farewells were the worst time of the week.

For John, things were going from bad to worse. By now Hattie was at the end of her tether, sometimes when I was invited to dinner at Eardley Crescent the tension in the house was like a fine mist settling over John's misery. Only their boys, Robin and Kim, seemed impervious, both being at that age when their own mysterious pre-occupations filled most of their time. As often happens in such strained marital situations, they were spoiled both by John and Hattie as the parents attempted to compensate for the atmosphere and for the times they were working away. At least John was getting masses of work, some of which cheered him up when he was out of town, but little lifted his gloom when he was at home. Kim and Robin accepted Scofield's constant presence as quite normal in the busy household. Happily they liked me as well: I knew about boys and I would tell them blatant lies such as whispering that I was a private detective working on a secret case of national importance. They lapped it up like gullible puppies and remembered all my lies afterwards. They seemed to be coping rather well with this odd family situation but deep down it must have been confusing for them and I have often hoped that not too much psychological damage was done.

And so the year turned, Christmas came with the practical gift of an electric blanket from John to warm my mostly celibate bed. Working in the Establishment did give rise to the odd encounter, usually with a feckless musician or an actor with problems. Such charming impossibles seemed to head for my bosom with some regularity and, of course, I found them more interesting and appealing than most other men.

One night in early May during a lull at the club, John was talking to Heawood and me, bemoaning that he was off to Greece in a few days to do a film called *In the Cool of the Day* starring Peter Finch and Jane Fonda. He didn't like the script and he didn't want to go to Greece. 'Oh, John,' said Heawood, 'just think of the culture, and the scenery and all those men dancing together.' 'In that case,' said John, 'perhaps old Peter Finch and I will have a slow waltz around the Parthenon.' As it turned out his fears were groundless. His part was that of a Persian doctor and John had already told Freddie Joachim that, casting-wise, this was going a bit far. He had even suggested two other actors on Freddie's books who would have done a much better job. He hated every minute of the film and sent me a postcard saying that he was quite awful in the part. Peter Finch was going through a bad patch and Jane Fonda was just a little precious – taking at least four hours in make-up, which left co-star Angela Lansbury to work her customary magic as comforter and friend. John had worked with Angela Lansbury before and he adored her. I think her father was something grand like a politician if memory serves me right, but John told me that she was the most unaffected and down-to-earth person off stage and such a star as soon as she stepped into the spotlight.

I don't have that card any more or by any means all of the notes and letters he sent me over the years when he was working away, but I do have a fair few. How I wish I'd kept more, but one can't hoard everything and memory can serve for the most part.

On his return he told me that one night he did venture up to the Parthenon and on the way he began to realize why the ancient Greeks were such good athletes. There was a full moon and some sort of *son et lumière* festival going on, with people in fancy dress and masked. He struck up conversation with an exotic creature who told him that she was a Greek actress. He asked her to reveal her face but she replied, 'Not until dawn.' When she did he discovered that she had a cast in one eye and more than a hint of a moustache. So he trundled off down the hill as day broke.

His next film was *The Punch and Judy Man* starring Tony Hancock and this was more up his street. Tony was a close friend and John had worked with him on lots of *Hancock's Half Hours*, quite the most popular BBC light entertainment pro-gramme of its time. Hattie had played his landlady in the radio version, so he was really at home. The trouble was that Tony's marriage was also going through a bad patch and instead of cheering and supporting each other they were doing a lot of commiserating, often well lubricated, in clubs and bars.

However, he was always able to enjoy moments of lightness.

Royal Albion Hotel
Brighton
Wednesday, May 6th 1964

Hullo love,

I am off in the morning, drifting along the coast and ending up at Margate for a couple of nights.

Many curious and funny things have happened to me of which I will tell you when I see you, for your information your telephone would appear to be out of order! I have tried twice, and that is what 'they' say.

Last night I went to the opening of a play that Eli Wallach and his wife are in. It was a wonderful evening in the theatre and I went round for a moment to pay my respects, he is such a darling and so is his wife whom I had not met.

You will *not* believe this but I swear it is true. I was talking to the manager of the theatre and John Gielgud, when I noticed out of the corner of my eye that the door of the loo out of which I had emerged a moment previously had not closed properly. In sight of all who cared to look was a gentleman wearing a flowered chiffon cape *over* a very ordinary suit, *pissing* into the *basin*. This is the truth I promise – I couldn't really make it up. I pointed it out to Gillie (the manager) who had his back turned to the proceedings, who immediately had a small fit or seizure.

I don't think Gielgud saw,
I had to laugh as they say.

Love,

John xx

On 10 June 1964 things changed. I say now that the change came suddenly, unexpectedly without forethought, but how can I be sure? I heard a writer being interviewed on the radio the other day. He was saying that all autobiography is fiction because one only selects moments to keep, all the details get blown away and forgotten. My memory lane is long and overgrown and this moment happened almost thirty-seven years ago.

It was David's seventh birthday and I had arranged my summer holidays to be with him. Sheila had come to Ramsgate for the weekend and as it was a beautiful day we packed a picnic and took David and a bunch of his friends to the West Cliff beach. We were right in the thick of the party when John suddenly appeared. This surprised me for two reasons: firstly, John never turned up unexpectedly, and secondly he never went to the beach. Feeling some great need to see me he had taken the trouble to come all the way down to Ramsgate, called at the house and had been directed here by my mother.

He was dreadfully depressed, having come straight from visiting Tony Hancock and their 'commiserating' had left them not only feeling sorry for each other but sorry for themselves. To cheer himself up he took Sheila and me out to Ramsgate's finest for dinner that night and later to a drinking club where he was collared by a fan. While they were talking I watched John dispassionately and, for the first time, it struck me how attractive he was with his broad shoulders and aristocratic features. He looked up suddenly and caught my appraising eye. In that moment everything changed between us. Another dimension had been added to our relationship, a new and very exciting one.

A strange sequence of coincidence began that night. Sheila, for some reason I can't now remember, was staying at a house in London Road that weekend – either a bed and breakfast place or a friend's home. When we dropped her outside we watched her walk down the sloping path to the front door and waited until she was safely inside, then John and I kissed properly for the first time. Nothing was said. John drove around until we found a place private enough for us to make love as had been on both our minds since that moment when we had looked at each other differently. Many years later we bought that house in London Road in front of which John had first kissed me and from whence the ambulance took him away to die.

3

When John and I became lovers he was spurred to get out of Eardley Crescent after fourteen years and strike out for himself. He found what he needed in Barons Court, west London, in a horseshoe-shaped block of flats called Barons Keep, which faced the playing fields of St Paul's School. It was near the tube station, one stop from Earls Court and had the advantage of a bar and restaurant on the ground floor. A relieved Hattie selected appropriate pieces of furniture from Eardley Crescent and just before Christmas 1964 John moved in.

On moving day I went straight from work to help him unpack and found him in the most hopeless muddle. The bed was in the bedroom and the fridge in the kitchen, so he'd got that right, but he hadn't a clue about where the rest of the furniture ought to belong. I was moved by his helplessness and I knew then that I would have to care for him. By the time I'd rearranged things, it was a home with a bit of me in it and I could see all sorts of things I could do to make it look even better. Later that evening, to celebrate the first day of his new life, he took me to dinner in Kensington and over an extravagant and boozy meal he asked me to give up my job and move in with him. I did.

At first I found that giving up work was a bigger wrench than I could have imagined, not for the work itself, but because it represented my independence and freedom. To compensate, John was easy to live with. He immediately turned his affairs over to me, his money was put into a joint account and from that day on I doubt that he ever looked at a bank statement. With Hattie's help I opened accounts at Derry & Toms, Barkers and an excellent wine merchants called Norton & Langridge. I only had to pick up a phone and everything was delivered. Hattie, seeing how little I had to do did not let me be idle for long. She had rented two charity shops which sold second-hand clothes and bric-à-brac to raise money for leukaemia research, so I worked there with her for two or three days a week and we grew even closer with so much time to share. She was happy at the time: she had her man at her side and it was to last for another few years. She was in demand professionally working on the Sykes comedy series and the Carry Ons, John was settled and contented and all three of our sons had accepted and approved of our new living arrangements.

The spring of 1965 found John in the South of France for a film called *The Liquidators* with Akim Tamiroff.

Hotel Negresco
Nice
Tues-wed 1965

My darling Joanie,

I am missing you a lot and often think of you and how much you would like it here. I didn't realize how rocky the coast was, you hardly see any sand in fact you have to import it at Cannes, the beach here is only shingle like at Brighton.

Today was another cloudy overcast morning though the wind has dropped so we went back to the villa to continue where we had left off, as it were, Tamiroff and I rehearsed a scene and everything was ready for it to be shot, when the sun came out and looked like staying out, so we had to abandon for the time being our scene and the unit moved outside to do some helicopter shots and I got back to the hotel at about 3.30.

I am sleeping well and have no need for pills though I wake rather early, have been having breakfast in my room at 7 a.m. just coffee and croissants.

The children and Jo sent a cable for my birthday but I did not do anything special, someone gave me a half bottle of champagne, which was kind of him but I don't really like the stuff, as you know.

I feel quite tired at the end of the day and got to bed around 11.00 take care of yourself my darling, I long to see you and hear from you.

More than ever.

John xx

Hotel Negresco
Nice
Sunday
1965

I am worried that I have not heard from you darling. Maybe there is a strike or you have been busy, I know you were during the early part of the week.

I shall be glad to be back on the whole, I miss you very much and am a bit lonely from time to time and of course everything is so wildly expensive.

I walked for about five miles today, it was cloudy and windy but I felt it doing me good.

I went to the old part of Nice, round the harbour, the architecture in that district is rather Italian in style and quite different from this expensive golden mile we inhabit.

I may be back for Easter as I have finished most of what I am required to do, in any case darling I will send a wire to you at Ramsgate if you are not at home when I get back. It seems ages since last Sunday. This morning I sat on the terrace of this hotel reading *The Country Girl*, and looking up every now and then at all the people passing by then going back to the book, I found the book very poignant and touching.

Yesterday we were at Monte Carlo and by a swimming pool at a hotel at Beaulieu, you would have loved it as it was a beautiful day, there were 50 or so bikini clad girls, many of whom were variations on a theme of Bardot, but also there were some milk chocolate coloured ones, all about 19 years old but not as engaging as you.

Such are the prices on this coastline, if one spent £50 a day you would not be overdoing it or in any way living it up.

A shirt costs 7/6p to be laundered! However, its nice to have been brought here and they seem pleased with me and I think I told you how much I enjoyed working with Tamiroff – we really got on as actors, sort of 'Clicked' like David Niven and I did.

Incidentally, someone pointed out to me his villa on Cap Ferrat, it looked beautiful with lovely grounds; I wish he had been there. I am not working tomorrow (Monday) but on Tuesday I am at Nice airport and sometime we have to do my arrival at the villa, which is a night shot – and that is it so far as I can see until I do that bit at the studio, darling would you send love to Ron and Audrey, I don't know their address or their second name come to that.

My love to you as always,

John xx

Not long after I moved in to Barons Keep a bigger flat became vacant next door to ours and we took it on. It had large sunny rooms and a balcony where the following summer I planted out geraniums and petunias. We acquired a cleaner called Lynn, not so much a Mrs Mop as a dear old Mrs Malaprop, who used to get her words wrong and say things like 'creased lightning' and 'congratulated iron'. Once after spotting a picture of the Pope in the newspaper she muttered, 'He's nobody special, his father was only a pheasant.' John adored her, his ear was always cocked for one of her gems, which would send him into hiding behind his newspaper shaking with silent laughter. We returned from holiday in Ibiza one year with a painting of the crucifixion. Lynn looked at it for a long time before saying, 'Wasn't that a shame?'

John was anxious to get married and we all agreed to let Hattie take proceedings against us on the grounds of his adultery with me. In 1965 we were still living in the dark ages when even a person as well-loved as Hattie might have been harmed professionally by disclosing the true facts, so the proceedings cast her in the role of victim, which she never was. She and Scofield were also eager to marry so we obtained a double divorce on the same day, with me divorcing Mark on the grounds of his desertion. It was arranged between our solicitors that Hattie's case was heard first and I was allowed to stand at the back the courtroom while her decree was granted. Obviously in the eyes of the law we were antagonists: I was the younger model who had wrecked her marriage, so we couldn't smile or acknowledge each other but as she left the courtroom staring straight ahead, she blew me a kiss. Hattie and the boys wrote to us and I have kept these letters, which we both treasured, all these years.

Dear Daddy and Joan

I am really so glad that you are getting married, because I love you very much. I hope you are very happy together, I know that Kim and I will like it a lot.

All my love,

Robin

Dear daddy and Joan

I hope you both have a happy marriage, it's a lovely idea.

I love you both a lot.

Kim

Hattie Jacques
67 Eardley crescent
SW5

Dear Johnny

Thank you for telling me your news, I do feel I would like to tell you that truly and sincerely I wish for your happiness, for your peace of mind and for everything to be good in your future marriage.

Joan is a lovely person who I know understands and loves you and is so much better for you than I could ever have been.

We have all been through a pretty wretched time but out of it all I'm sure will come great happiness for all of us.

God bless and my love.

Jo

We made the front page of the *Evening Standard* that night. Under my photo – in which, incidentally, I looked very chic in a suit and a hat – it said, 'The other woman' which we expected, and the story went on to dismiss my affair with John as being a nine-day wonder. Later that day John, Hattie, John Scofield and I assembled at Eardley Crescent and over a glass or two of champagne we toasted each other's futures. What a pity the press were not there to take some more photos.

John and I married on 2 March 1966 at Fulham Town Hall with Bruce Copp as our best man. When we drew up outside there was a banner over the entrance announcing that the local operatic society was presenting a production of *Bless the Bride*, which I took to be a good omen. It was a quiet little wedding. Beside Bruce Copp the other guests were Marty and Loretta Feldman and Sheila. We had lunch in the same restaurant where John had proposed, Tratoo in Abingdon Road off Kensington High Street. The place still thrives, I understand. We got drunk on champagne and John went to the piano and played 'What's New?' which made everybody laugh, this being his third attempt at marriage.

The following morning at 6.00 a.m. and suffering from bad champagne hangovers we were at Euston where we caught the early train to Manchester. John was to do a pilot comedy play for ITV with Warren Mitchell. I don't think the project ever progressed from there. I do remember clearly that Warren was about to start on a new series called *Till Death Us Do Part* and on the journey to Manchester he regaled us with a description of the Alf Garnett character whom he was to portray so brilliantly in the coming years.

While I was in Manchester on my honeymoon I made a nostalgic visit to Oldham to visit my aunts, who were still living in the same houses in the same streets as they had all those years ago. Our old house was still there, although by now it was a smart bakery. I looked up at the window of the room where Grandma had died and said a little prayer for her. Then I went to find the Lyric cinema but it had gone and a modern block of flats was standing in its place. Later I took my aunts and cousins to lunch in Oldham and got them all tight and on the day of the recording John got them all passes for his show. We had laid on a buffet supper for them afterwards and although John and Warren had just finished a transmission they were kindness itself to my relatives. When I left Manchester I felt that I had exorcised a ghost from the past. I've never been back; all my aunts and uncles are dead now, and my cousins are all grand-mothers like me. I'm sure my relatives never forgot that meeting with John: for a start it was their first brush with fame and then meeting Warren Mitchell as well made it a double thrill for them. But what I'm sure thrilled them more was the fact that 'Our Joan' had married a real gent who loved and cared for her.

Mum and Dad adored him not for his celebrity but for his steadfastness and his devotion – which was soon to be tested to the limit. David, who naturally loved his handsome swash-buckling father, had been upset at first when we got divorced. He couldn't see why I wanted to marry an old man like John, as he saw him. But over the years they became real friends and to David, John's constancy and gentleness became the rock that he knew he could always depend on.

That spring and summer of 1966 were a happy time for us. John was much in de-mand for films which, truthfully, were forgettable but great fun at the time. Just before our marriage we had spent six happy weeks in Morocco where he was cast in *Our Man in Marrakech*. It had a large and varied cast headed by Tony Randall, a lovely Broadway actor who usually played second lead in Hollywood films, alongside, for example, such stars as Rock Hudson and Doris Day. He was supported by Wilfrid Hyde-White, Terry-Thomas, Herbert Lom, Klaus Kinski and a gorgeous German actress called Senta Berger. We all got on well together, but it was Wilfrid who became a special friend and we had dinner together almost every night as he was on his own. No one could have asked for better company – for all his idiosyncrasies. He was always cold and even in the heat of Morocco he wore a waistcoat, overcoat and scarf. Wrapped up in this fashion he would sit by the hotel pool enjoying a drink with John while I swam, regaled by his pleas not to catch my death in 90 degrees Fahrenheit.

Terry-Thomas, another cast member, once asked me to dress up as a Moroccan woman in black robes and yashmak and pose for some publicity photos. Afterwards, still wearing the costume, I found John and Wilfrid having their usual lunch-time drinks by the pool. I didn't speak, I simply stared at them. 'What's the matter, dear?' asked

Wilfrid. I continued to stare in silence. 'You try and see what she wants, Johnny,' said Wilfrid. 'Perhaps she wants money,' said John and held some out to me. I jumped back as if horrified. 'Oh dear, I hate to be rude to these people, but I wish I knew the Moroccan for "Fuck Off",' said Wilfrid. I blew a loud raspberry at them from under my yashmak and left, to exclamations of 'How extraordinary,' from John and 'Bloody rude if you ask me,' from Wilfrid.

Marrakech was a city of extremes, the contrast between the poor and the so-called elite being appalling. I felt shame at living in a luxury hotel when always at the gates were beggars, street vendors, crippled children in rags being pushed forward by their elders to beg. One morning as I left the hotel I was horrified by the sight of two men holding out a dead baby towards me. They were wailing and obviously asking me for money to bury the poor little thing. I ran away in tears and when I arrived at the location the first person I saw was Wilfrid. 'My dear girl, whatever is the matter?' he asked, shocked at my distress. I sobbed out my story; there was a long pause. 'Oh dear me,' said Wilfrid, 'for sale I suppose.' His outrageous remark had the desired effect and I laughed. He mitigated this seeming heartlessness by pointing out that the poor little soul was probably in better hands than it had ever been in life. We never lost touch with Willy, as John affectionately called him, and met up with him every time he came to England.

Years later we visited him in Los Angeles, while we were staying with John's son Robin. It was Christmas Eve and Wilfrid was quite ill. Divorced from his wife, Ethel, and estranged from his family, he was being cared for by a sort of gay nurse-minder with whom he seemed to get on well in a bantering and complaining sort of way. We had intended to stay for an hour but Wilfrid wanted us to stay longer. 'Be kind,' he said at one point, 'I don't often get any proper company.' He was enjoying himself ambling with John through the past. It seemed so sad that someone so essentially English should be in exile in America. We asked him about his children – I think there were two of them by his young former wife. 'Don't ever have any American children, Johnny,' he said. 'They're very odd.' We gathered that there was little contact between them. He kept asking his carer to fetch us drinks and when I refused alcohol, it being early in the day, he asked, 'What about those funny cigarettes, then, do you like them? Because he certainly does,' indicating his minder friend, and adding, 'Go on, roll some up for her.' He was eager to have our company and it was impossible to refuse so we stayed on for a couple more hours while he and John swapped yarns and I listened, happily puffing away at my funny cigarettes. We never saw him again. He moved to Palm Springs for the heat. An Englishman to the core except that he could not bear the cold.

Although John and I were in some ways an oddly matched couple we both liked being married to each other. John gave me free rein in the home: I decorated as I pleased, choosing furniture, curtains, anything I wanted for the flat, without him showing the slightest interest. Through John, Hattie and general osmosis I developed some taste, I hope. The only thing he ever noticed was if I had moved a painting: pictures were his domain. Hattie once said that if there was a pig tethered in the hall he would step over it to straighten a picture. When we visited friends' homes it was only the paintings that he saw although it also worried him if there were no bookcases. He said you could find out everything about a person by their pictures and their books.

He always introduced me as 'my friend who is also my wife'. And we *were* good friends, not the kind who wormed out the secrets of each other's souls but the kind who respect each other's freedom and privacy. If he was more morose than usual the reason would be revealed in a throw-away line during a conversation about something else. The secret was not to go digging like a dog worrying a bone. He was simply not a confrontational person, unlike me, so there was some adjusting to do as there is in every relationship, but really very little.

We did not stifle each other. I didn't always go with him when he had to travel to film or TV locations – hence all the cards and notes he sent me over the years. He didn't always feel obliged to accompany me when I went back to Ramsgate to visit David and my parents. All in all we rubbed along very well and had a perfectly satis-factory sex life, thank you. Our marriage was good, free, contented, no shocks or alarms, and it continued on its serene way for what seemed like a happy eternity but which was only a very short time really. Tony Hancock changed everything.

4

It was September 1966 and John and I had been married for just six months.

The telephone rang on a Sunday evening while I was preparing dinner and John was watching TV, a cosy domestic scene. John answered it and came into the kitchen to say there would be one more for dinner. Tony's new marriage to Freddie Ross, his publicist, was in ruins after just three months; he was in a bad way and needed company. I remember thinking, what a bloody nuisance. There was something I had wanted to watch on TV and I was in the mood for a quiet night. That's all. I had liked Tony during the couple of evenings John and I had spent with him before, but knew he could be tiring company. Oh well. I wondered if the food would stretch...

John went off to pick up his friend and bring him into our peaceful home. Within three weeks of that night, Tony and I had fallen in love, I had left my husband, our home and my reason behind and embarked on a two-year affair which ended with Tony's suicide in a lonely flat in Sydney, Australia. People do fall when they love that intensely. They fall under a spell where there is no reality or sense.

Shakespeare wrote, 'Love is a smoke made from the fume of sighs.' During those two years there was much sighing and weeping and drama. We were drenched in guilt and consumed by love and passion all at the same time. It didn't help that Tony's drinking was out of control. Time and time again he began cures and dry-outs, and each time he fell off the wagon and let it roll over him. I went from hope to despair like a metronome and while Tony and I were knocking the hell out of each other mentally and spiritually, John, amazingly, was my support and safe harbour. His love for us both gave him the courage and understanding to cope with the unbearable. We never discussed divorce. The way patience and love and hope had just about sustained him during the darkest days of his marriage to Hattie was a strength he was able to muster again.

Hattie was as usual a comfort: who better to understand what had happened to me. She said, 'Open hearts are easily invaded,' when I was with her one day and trying to make some sense of why we had both behaved in the same way and hurt John so badly. She was always there on the end of the phone to give me help and advice when Tony went off the rails. Bruce Copp and John Heawood were also staunch and unjudgemental allies. They knew Tony from the days when they were all starting out together and understood his complex and vulnerable nature. But there were others who never forgave me, some people in the business who had worked with John regarded him with such affection that I was doubly condemned. I can't say I could blame them.

After the first year of our affair and after his drinking had accelerated to an unbearable peak – culminating in his driving me away for fear that he might harm me – I moved back into John's life saying, and believing at the time, that it was all over between Tony and me. Mercifully his agent at Bernard Delfont's office had found Tony a cabaret season in Australia which he took off for. Apart from reading an account in the newspapers which had upset me terribly, that he had fallen off the stage during his act one night after a drinking session with Matt Monroe, I began to ease back into my peaceful life with John.

But one Sunday evening when John was away filming and I was in Ramsgate with David, it all began again. A famous chat show was on TV, advertised as having a mystery guest. For some reason I had a premonition that it would be Tony. Of course, it was. There he was on screen looking fit, in command, and back to his old lovable brilliance. While we were watching this David, who adored Hancock, whispered, 'Tony rang this morning wanting to speak to you and Nana said you weren't here.' Needless to say my parents had been devastated at the break-up of my happy marriage to John, whom they loved dearly, and although Tony had won them over for a while, his drinking had appalled them. It had been a great relief to them when I had resumed my life with John.

The next morning – while my parents were out – Tony rang again. When I picked up the phone the first thing he said was, 'I've been praying for the sound of your voice, will you come back to me?' I told him I couldn't, I was with John and I couldn't hurt him again. When we had first collided Tony and I were both so sure of our love for each other that we decided we couldn't conduct an illicit affair and felt that it was more honest to own up and face the music. This time it was different. I was certain from the past year's experience that his drinking would always be an unpredictable element in our lives. So I didn't leave John again, but Tony and I would meet in secret and grab whatever opportunity to be together presented itself. And during that second year I lived two lives and ran two homes. When John left for work I would run to Tony, and when John was away we would spend nights together hiding away from public places for the fear of being spotted. If John had any doubts during that time – and I'm sure he did – he never let them show, and never asked a question that he didn't want an answer to. It was both a terrible time and a wonderful time. Tony even went on the wagon and vowed to earn my trust by staying on it. The time we spent together then was of a deeper and more loving quality than ever before.

In the spring of 1968 he was offered the chance of a television series in Australia. It was to be his big comeback and he accepted. He was to be away for three months at least, and we arranged that he would write to me via a PO box and we would phone whenever the possibility arose. I saw him off at Victoria Station on 22 March after risking the last night with him on some pretence of staying with a friend, and promised him that if he could stay sober for one year I would leave John and marry him.

During the first six weeks he wrote regularly, even sending post cards en route and I replied promptly. In his letters he begged me to stay strong and believe in him, and I assured him I would.

Then things began to go wrong. I never knew the details until as recently as two years ago when I met Eddie Joffe who was his director on the series and became his friend and confidant. We met at a Tony Hancock Appreciation Society dinner in Bournemouth. The dinner was held in the hotel that had previously been owned by Tony's parents and where he spent a good part of his youth. It was a strange experience being in a place where he had actually lived, and even stranger to be introduced to Eddie, especially when his first words were, 'I've been waiting to meet you for twenty-eight years.' After the dinner Eddie and I went into the bar and he told me about those months up to Tony's death. He was writing a book about it called *Hancock's Last Stand* and together we pieced together the missing parts. We have stayed in touch ever since, and I subsequently received his book. It is crafted with honesty, compassion and love. He said that when he found Tony dead on that awful morning after receiving no answer to his usual wake-up call, his first impression was that he had never noticed how blue his eyes were. I knew, and I also knew that when he was happy they were bright clear blue, and when he was sad or angry they were grey.

Eddie also gave me an envelope containing the letters I had written in answer to Tony's. I dreaded to see what an immature and illiterate writer I had been, and was reluctant to awaken sad memories. They were embarrassing at times, but not sloppy – neither of us was – more shy really. But the love came through and touched me with feelings I had buried. They are now put away with his. I don't know what to do with them really – to strangers they would mean nothing.

Although Tony never disclosed my name to Eddie, he talked of me incessantly and Eddie said he carried my letters everywhere, quoting bits to him. The producer of the

Australian series was evidently a man with no concept of Tony's sensitive nature and his deep lack of self worth. They crossed swords and Tony, knowing that the series wasn't working, went back on the booze in a big way. At the same time there was a nationwide postal strike in Australia and my last few letters did not reach him. Convinced that I had ceased to care for him he rang his mother asking her to find me and arrange for us to talk. Sadly, when his mother rang my flat I was out shopping and missed her call. She then rang my Ramsgate number. My mother answered and, horrified to hear that Tony was trying to contact me, said that I was in Rome with John and wanted nothing to do with Tony.

That night, convinced that his career and our affair were both over, he took an overdose. Still protecting me, he left Eddie a note and one to his mother, saying that too many things had gone wrong and reminding her that the soul was immortal.

The following morning the phone rang early. I was still asleep, but John answered it. He heard the news from his agent Peter Campbell, who had heard it on the radio. When John woke me to tell me the awful news I was unable to hide my grief, and it all came out. Poor John had to deal with my heartbreak and inconsolable pain, as well as my treachery. But he did deal with it and when I emerged into the light and saw how blessed I was, he gave me strength to deal with it as well.

There was an occasion in a theatrical club a year after Tony's suicide, while I was still shaken by his death, when a well-known character actor much the worse for drink called me 'a tart and a trollop for hurting lovely John with that bastard Hancock'. Before I could speak in my own defence John roared in reply with a ferocity I had never seen before: 'How dare you speak to my wife in that way? What do you know of others' feelings, you insensitive little turd. If I ever hear you speak to my wife or any other woman in that manner, I'll knock your teeth down your throat.' Then he took my arm and escorted me out. It was as if the place had turned to stone. People stood, frozen as statues with drinks and fags half-way to mouths as we left in a pin-dropping silence. It was only afterwards that John began to shake, and later at home over a large brandy apiece I told him how proud I was of him. He was dismissive and said any man would have done the same.

But not any man would have. He treated me during that entire episode of our lives, not only during the ugly scene that night in the club, with just the same constancy he had always shown, as if I were an invalid recovering from a serious illness. All that brave grace put the foundations of our marriage on to a sound and consequently unbreakable path. In many ways we had remained together during my affair with Tony, and certainly divorce never seemed to be on the agenda when I loved him so much and while we remained – against all the odds – able to care for each other in practical ways.

Afterwards Tony's shadow was always there, but not between us, more like something that united us. There would always be a scar and he will never be forgotten. John said that if it taught him anything it was never to take anyone or anything for granted because people and love and life could be snatched away at any time. I could write much more about Tony but this book is not about him, it is about John and the letters he wrote and received during the good years that came after that tragic beginning. They will reveal more about him than I ever could. The most I can hope for is to complete some unfinished business and reply at last to all those lovely but unanswered letters.

5

Although John wrote often during our courtship most of the letters have been lost. He was never one to write to me flowery love letters, but the 'miss you' at the end spoke volumes, as did the fact that he was trying to cut down on his smoking in order to impress me. He failed miserably in this department. Like Hattie, he was practically a chain-smoker. Years later when he was working with Noël Coward on *The Italian Job*, the Maestro, who was also a heavy smoker, asked him how many a day he smoked. 'Ninety-two,' said John. 'Not nearly enough,' replied Noël.

This is one of the earliest letters, written before we were married.

Sunday

Hello darling,

I am writing this at my father's desk, which is wide and comfortable and serenely pleasant.

I am surrounded by pictures of me in various films, also one at the age of seven, and some lovely ones of the children, which I had forgotten about.

It is fairly late and I'm pleasantly tired after the drive down. Stopped at Newmarket (no cigarettes all the way from London) and went into the Rutland Arms washed with a piece of kitchen table soap, had a glorious pissola, a drink, and then phoned my mother telling her that I was half an hours drive away.

'I'm All Right Jack' is on in the town and in the bar were some people who had just come from it and one young man who was just going to it; He is studying work management which incorporates 'Time and Motion' and the film had been shown to him on a course of instruction he had been attending, it amused him so much he was off to catch it once more.

Not an unpleasant interlude as it turned out.

Hope work goes well with you,

Try to keep Wednesday free; I will call you when I get back.

Miss you.
Love John

Not long after writing this John took me to meet his mother. He wanted to show me where he had spent most of his childhood and we also stopped off at the Rutland Arms for a drink and a wash and brush-up. I was feeling apprehensive and rather shy about meeting his mum. John had told me next to nothing about her as it was not his way to draw character sketches of people or to go into deep analytical reasons about why they were as they were. He either liked them or he didn't.

I remember being slightly nervous about the fact that I came from a different class and I wondered if it would be obvious or matter to her. I need not have worried as, far from being intimidating, she was as shy and gentle as John and seemed pleased to know that there was someone in his life who was making him happy. It was a lovely visit if a short one. John had booked us into a hotel in the town, intending to spend a few days showing me the countryside and visiting a few stables. His love of the turf – everything about the experience of the races – never lessened. But, blast it, within a few hours of our arrival Freddie rang to say that a very lucrative TV commercial might be available

117

if he had a voice test so we had to go back to London immediately.

I never had the opportunity to meet John's mother again as she died soon afterwards, but I remember that afternoon with great affection for the graciousness of both her welcome and her home. The house was beautiful and serene like her, and left me with the impression of a taste and a lifestyle that I could only aspire to acquiring in later life. It also gave me a deeper insight into the influences that made John the kind of man he was – imbued with an unshakeable confidence that would serve him well whatever life hurled at him and, perhaps most importantly, the sense that he never had a need to compete. He knew who he was and where he came from. I would have loved her to be my mother-in-law but when I met her the idea of marriage was still some way off. John never got the sugar commercial either, dammit.

Happily, after the sadness of the two previous years and as a just reward for all John had endured, at the end of 1968 fate threw him a little blessing by the name of *Dad's Army*.

He did not see it that way at first, it was

just another job by which to earn his crust and have enough left for the best butter. But Clive Dunn was already lined up which was a bonus as they were old friends from almost twenty years earlier at the Players' Theatre, where John had met and married Hattie and Clive had met and married Cilla Morgan. When he was first approached about *Dad's Army* and read the script he found it rather dull. There was no love interest and no glamour. He held out little hope for its success and told his agent that he would only do it if Clive was definitely on for it too. Neither of them gave much to the chances of a pilot for a putative TV comedy series pivoting around a bunch of old men in Britain's wartime home guard.

The idea was that the platoon was based in a small south coast town during the post-Dunkirk period of the Second World War when alarmists spoke of Nazi invasion every day, Britain was scrimping and pinching on dreadful rations and the old boys in the platoon didn't even have proper rifles with which to repel the enemy. Actually there was one young man in *Dad's Army*, Private Pike, who was too delicate to join the army proper and whose mummy (who also happened to be John's character's middle-aged popsy), always made sure he wore a woolly scarf when on parade. Clive had the same doubts and said the same thing: he would only do it if John enlisted, so to speak. So this TV classic began without a particularly confident fanfare of enthusiasm as the company gathered for the first rehearsal.

The principal, absolute and – as it has proved – enduring genius underpinning the programme was that of writers Jimmy Perry and David Croft. As well as turning very funny and neat storylines they managed to imbue all the favourite British vices and virtues in one inefficient platoon, week after week. Snobbery, deflation of pomposity, sympathy for the underdog, fear of the foreign, mistrust of authority yet a strange yielding to it, courage, cowardice, incompetence, silly vicars, muddle, fair play and getting away with a lucky break... The list could go on. The second stroke of genius lay in the inspired casting of a show which has become as much of a fixture of British TV, thirty years on, as the American classic Sergeant Bilko.

Most of the cast were old troupers, seasoned players who had been around too long to bring much enthusiasm to bear upon the project initially, none of them thinking that it would run after the first six episodes. After all, who would really care about a comedy set in drabbest wartime England centring around a vicar and a bad-tempered air-raid warden whose real war was with the hopeless old soldiers who commandeered the parish hall? Surely the formula for success demanded a heart-throb lead at least and a bit of love interest, not this shuffling band of khaki-clad codgers led by an insufferably pompous bank manager who lied about his First World War record?

It was a few weeks before John began cautiously to enjoy it. His casting as Sergeant Wilson was brilliant – the laconic, educated and utterly unambitious chap who is quite content to play second fiddle to Captain Mainwaring both in bank and platoon. The whole cast got on well together from the start. One actor who does not merge in with the rest, be it a cast of thousands or a small team, can sour the whole thing, but there was none of that in *Dad's Army*. In James Beck for instance, who played the spivvy but utterly charming Private Walker who could always find a girl a pair of nylons – at a price – John found a real best friend. Most afternoons after

121

rehearsal I would find them at home together when I came in from shopping,
having a laugh and unwinding over a couple
of drinks.

John found Jimmy easy to confide in. He
was unshockable and open-minded and,
like Clive Dunn, he had no axe to grind on
the subject of my transgression with Tony,
so I too was able to talk to him as a friend
who understood that life contained many
pitfalls and pratfalls and that falling in love
wasn't the worst sin in the world. In fact the
whole cast were kind and generous to me
and drew me into their circle. It was a family
affair, *Dad's Army*, and we all grew very
close, wives included.

Out of all the wives Cilla Dunn and Kay
Beck were the two of whom I saw the most.
We all lived within a stone's throw of each
other in London and, of course, Cilla and I
had known each other before *Dad's Army*.
Jimmy Beck would pick John up from our
Barons Keep flat each morning for rehearsals and often when he dropped John back
Kay would come over and stay for dinner or
we might go back to their place to eat – Kay
was a marvellous cook. Then again, sometimes we would go out to dine. Whatever we
did during those happy years we did it mob-

handed, so to speak. On location we got even closer: Kay and I would sometimes take the train up to Thetford where location sequences were filmed and have a sort of holiday with our husbands. During the day when the men were working, Kay would drive me out sightseeing in the lovely Norfolk countryside. Joan Lowe, however, was always with Arthur: they were never apart, virtually joined at the hip, but even if we didn't get quite so close we all liked each other well enough.

All the cast members loved the location work at Thetford. It was the honey on their bread and butter, and over the years a strong bond formed between the platoon and the locals (some of whom appeared in various episodes). John used to go off to Thetford driven either by Bill Pertwee or Jimmy Beck, both in a state of high excitement like children going off to the seaside rather than work. John had a special expression of endearment for dear Bill Pertwee, who loved a joke and still does. He was always making John laugh, sometimes when he shouldn't and John would say, 'I wish you'd learn to behave yourself, Billy.' It was rather like being in a gang, and we know how lads can be when they egg each other on.

One evening after work John was entertaining a rather stuffy old colonel and his wife in his hotel room. The colonel was a *Dad's Army* fan and John, polite as ever, was giving them drinks, helped by Jimmy, when the door was pushed open by Bill Pertwee wearing nothing save his warden's helmet and boots. 'Ready for a drink, John?' he said. Spotting the guests he leapt back into the hall and the safety of his room which was opposite. Quick as a flash Jimmy Beck dashed out ahead of him and slammed Bill's door, leaving him starkers and frantically looking for a place where he could cover his bits. He found the broom cupboard from where, red-faced and giggling, he beseeched Jimmy – who was by now helpless with laughter – to find the hall porter who had the pass key. The commotion outside the door died down and John's rather shocked visitors departed. John knocked at Bill's door. 'Who's there?' called Bill, by now suitably attired. 'You *know* who,' said John sternly. When Bill opened the door he barked, 'When will you learn to behave yourself, Billy?'

Every Friday night we congregated at the BBC for the taping of the show and during the warm-up, usually performed by Bill

Pertwee, we wives sat together and were introduced to the audience who applauded us as if we were part of the show, to our great embarrassment. I remember one time when Lynn, our beloved cleaning lady went along. It was in a week when I was in Ramsgate and John got tickets for her and her sister, both of them maiden ladies who adored John because he was so polite to Lynn, whose cleaning skills were only surpassed by her odd way with words and her eagerness to please. After seeing the show she said to John, 'That Bill Pertwee who did the warm-up, what a laugh! He ought to go on the stage.' She stayed with us for over ten years, all through the Hancock episode and beyond. She once gave us a tea service that she said was too good to leave to any of her relations as they were nothing but a bunch of tripe hounds and that I was to use it when my 'dainty' friends came to tea. That made John laugh. 'Are there any dainty people coming to tea today?' he would ask. Happy days.

In the autumn of 1975, by which time *Dad's Army* was established as one of Britain's top TV comedy shows, the cast were invited to switch on the Blackpool illuminations. Off we went, wives and all, for a jolly weekend. We had lunch on the train with enough wine to put us all in a festive mood and on arrival we were escorted to our hotel where, waiting for us in our rooms, we found a tin of biscuits and a stick of Blackpool rock apiece. 'A nice touch,' John said, with the merest lift of an eyebrow.

After changing – cast into uniforms, wives into evening wear – we went to the dining-room to meet the local dignitaries and were confronted by a meagre dinner before the ceremony of the lights. There was a notable lack of wine during the meal due, apparently, to a previous celebrity having over-indulged and made a mess of things during the switch-on. So after the hurried repast the men were all led off to the town hall, gasping for a drink, while we wives were also longing for something warm, inside and out, it being a cold night and us being in our flimsy finery. As I remember, while the cast did their little bit of business with Bill Pertwee shouting, 'Put that light out,' we civilians were herded into an ante-room which was freezing cold. Mercifully we were given a small nip of something, but we had to ask for it.

Once the deed was done, still separated from our menfolk we were taken to the point on the shore where the tramline began. *Dad's Army* cast in the front coach, ladies in the coach behind, we were then escorted by the Mayor and council members to be given the lovely if chilly honour of having first sight of the famous Blackpool illuminations. I remember little except being frozen and longing for a warm bar and a cold drink. At last we reached the end of the line and we were taken to the Winter Gardens to reunite with our men and hopefully be given a drink but they weren't finished with them yet. Into another ante-room we went – drinkless!

Here we were asked to form pairs and I was paired with Captain Mainwaring, Arthur Lowe, who by then was beginning to mutter ominously, which made me giggle. The doors of the ante-room were opened and to our combined horror we were all marched in pairs on to the stage of the Winter Gardens ballroom to the strains of 'Who do you think you are kidding, Mr Hitler'. The ballroom had great tableaux all round the mouldings of gnomes and fairy grottos and, as we were all being seated at a long table, Arthur said, 'Oh hello, it's the Ideal Gnome Exhibition.' Not a great joke, I grant you, but it started me giggling again.

The hall was full of people and on the long table laid out for our delight were plates of cake, slices of pork pie and coffee cups. Ominously, there were no glasses. Arthur called to an attendant and said in a sepulchral voice, 'Two large scotches here, please.' 'We're not allowed to serve doubles,' was the reply. 'In that case bring us two singles, then go away and bring us two more,' he ordered.

I couldn't meet John's eye during the ordeal of the 'long table'. We sat in a row being stared at by the audience, nibbling at our pork pies and Kunzel cakes – a popular pre-packaged turd-like thing. Arthur was sending it up out of the corner of his mouth and John's eyebrows were eloquent as ever. All of us found it ever more hilarious as the civic speeches went on. Arthur, who was very fond of his food, was taken by the excellence of the pork pies and enquired of the waiters where they could be purchased. The word had also gone around that there was a good night club in town so when, towards the end of the speeches, one of the dignitaries whispered to Arthur that we were invited to meet yet more of the local gentry, he said 'Not bloody likely. We've sung for our supper and now we're off to the

Lemon Tree.' We exited en masse and I hope the good people of Blackpool continue to enjoy *Dad's Army* and will forgive the telling of this little story.

We had a jolly time at the club where there was a jazz band, which pleased John, and we were made a great fuss of. In the end it turned out to be one of those special times that brought us all closer. Next morning, having secured some of the excellent pork pies we had enjoyed the previous evening, a slightly hungover bunch assembled for the return journey.

So many good times, and so much laughter over the years that I could go on remembering. There wasn't a member of the cast who hadn't a story. Holidaying with Clive Dunn and his family on the Algarve, for instance, had its moments. It says a great deal about friendship when people holiday together successfully and on several occasions we shared a villa without mishap. Polly Dunn, Clive's daughter, was John's special friend. She had adopted him at the age of six and always referred to him as 'Poor John' due to his woebegone expression. When he called at their house in Barnes, south-west London, as he did quite often, she instinctively knew that his first requirement would be a drink and she would mix lethal cocktails of anything that came to hand, while engaging in social pleasantries. She loved telling him ghost stories in a shaky voice and running her fingers over his face until he would plead, 'I'm so frightened, Polly, if you don't stop I shall have a small fit or seizure.' When she was just about old enough he took her to Ronnie Scott's to hear a jazz singer she liked and when he asked what she would like to drink she replied, 'I'll have a large gin and tonic please, John.'

One evening while we were sitting around the pool in the Algarve he said languidly, 'I always say this is the nicest part of the day,' and rolled fully dressed into the pool, much to Polly's delight.

'Oh you're so silly, John,' she said. 'You're wearing your clothes.'

'Good gracious, so I am,' he replied. So much for the stuffy and uptight upper middle-class Englishman.

I remember during one of our holidays a pack of dogs chasing a flighty little bitch on heat seemingly all over the Algarve. Wherever we went this bunch of randy canines would appear and one evening when we arrived back from the beach we found them all lying around the pool on the sun beds and towels, some having taken a dip so the water was now covered with a thick brown scum. Nothing had escaped, everything was marked by the terracotta coloured dust on their coats. Polly managed to get a snapshot of their retreating backs as they trotted off refreshed after their siesta, one or two looking back at us as if to say, 'Up yours, touristas.'

It was during the same holiday that we received a telegram from Arthur Lowe telling us of the death of Jimmy Beck. All laughter stopped then. We knew that he was dangerously ill and had been in a coma but none of us could accept the fact that he might die. He was opening a fete for some charity or other when he complained to Kay that he was feeling ill and he gave her the car keys, which Kay took to be serious as he always drove. Once they got home the doctor examined him and he was rushed in to hospital for an operation for a burst pancreas. He never recovered consciousness.

Kay never left him for one minute during the following three weeks: she slept, ate and bathed at the hospital and although she was told by the doctors that there was no hope at all, she never lost the belief that her will power and love would bring him back. Each morning at rehearsals Arthur would arrive with the latest news on Jimmy and pin it to the notice board: no change. It was inconceivable that someone as vital and funny as Jimmy could die when, with the exception of Ian Lavender, the rest of the cast were old men in comparison. It speaks well of the writers David Croft and Jimmy Perry that he was never replaced. These days in so many soaps and sit-coms we are asked to believe that a completely new face is really the same person who has been in the part for years. Think about the *Street* or *Emmerdale* over the years, but Jimmy could not be replaced with another wide boy or spiv character – he was unique.

Dear Kay could not replace him either. Although he died in 1969, over thirty years ago, there was never a hint of another man in her life. She was and is a stunningly beautiful woman, blonde and slim out of the Grace Kelly mould, and I know that she was sought after by quite a few admirers but to her there was only one Jimmy, and so say all of us who knew him.

Looking back I suppose we all seemed to react rather unemotionally to losing Jimmy, but the reality of his death was so stunningly horrendous, so tragic and wasteful there was nothing to say. He was only forty-four years old, a talented actor and a good friend. He had a sound marriage, a lovely wife and a promising future. We had seen him in several stage plays where his ability was stretched and proved way beyond the role of Private Walker, the spiv in *Dad's Army,* and yet suddenly, without warning it ended.

But who ever said life was fair...?

At the beginning of 1969 I found a home for us in Ramsgate. It was a bargain at £3500. A fairly large but unmodernized Victorian terraced house, it was garishly bright throughout – even the outside was painted in fuchsia and lilac – while inside each room was a riot of multi-patterned wallpapers and horrible swirly-whirly carpets. But the house was structurally sound and a classic architectural gem of its kind. I got all the right vibes and just knew that John and I could live there. It was not entirely selfish of me to have house-hunted around Ramsgate – John did have connections with the area through Hattie – but I cannot deny that I liked the idea of being near my parents and close to David who was twelve by then and settled in a local school. That windy corner of Kent has a definite charm, rather like a shabby, plain, yet defiant sister of super-glam Brighton along the coast to the west. The working port always gave it a bit of a bustle, appropriately enough for a Victorian town.

The only problem was that the journey to and from London was a bummer. In fact, to this day, while the train from Victoria to Brighton can take less than an hour, the train to Ramsgate takes twice as long through some of the dreariest reaches of English suburbia and 'countryside'. And if you drive you feel as if you're crossing Kansas. But finding that house in Grange Road felt like coming home for both of us. Years later we were to buy the house in London Road where, by strange coinci-dence, we had our first kiss by the gate, and where John lived until his death in 1995.

However, I still keep the house in Grange Road, which is full of happy memories as my parents lived there after us, and now it is my son David's future.

The house's previous owner was an old dear who had decided to sell up and see the world before she died so all her furniture, curtains and carpets were included in the price. Sadly, she had torn out all the original Victorian fireplaces, including a kitchen range in the basement, which she described as a huge monstrosity with a great over-mantel, several ovens and a big hearth. Nowadays, in the age of Aga, this alone would be worth more than twice what I originally paid for the whole house, but the widow was a product of a time which thought that anything Victorian was depressing and ugly. She had covered the stair rails and all the lovely old doors with flat, flush plywood and most of the ceilings with Styrofoam tiles. In short, she had tried to murder the place. Undeterred, I saw that it was still a bargain: it was scrupulously clean and from the top floor were marvellous views of Sandwich Bay and Deal. The old dear's hobby was cross-stitch and the walls of the house were covered with framed embroidered versions of distinguished pictures from Hals' *The Laughing Cavalier* to Constable's *Haywain*. To my great relief she told me that these were the only things she was taking with her and a quick sale was made. John took a cursory look at the house, wincing and shuddering, and said if I really wanted it all well and good.

It gave me an interest, something to take

my mind off the pain of the previous year so I threw myself into making it a home. Until then we had stayed with my parents during our visits to Ramsgate. We both loved the town and enjoyed getting away from the noise and chaos of London. Now we had a bolthole of our own. With the help of a local builder I knocked down a few walls, turning the warren of little dark rooms on the ground floor into larger light and airy ones. The front parlour had been the widow's pride and joy. The wallpaper had obviously been expensive with its raised pattern of cabbage roses in every shade of pink amid a trellis of powder blue. Over the fireplace was a beautiful mantelpiece with bevelled mirrors, shelves and a carved border – we certainly wanted to save that. Sadly the elderly vandal had painted it blue with a flaming pink trim which actually hurt the eyes. I set about the place with white paint and cream emulsion and painted over the cabbage roses without a pang of remorse.

A kindly new neighbour who had popped in to introduce herself and offer to help watched in horror as my roller obliterated all colour from the room. 'If Mrs King were dead,' she said, 'she'd turn in her grave if she saw what you're doing.' Well, you can't please everyone, I say, and when John next saw the house a few weeks later it was a cooler, calmer place with more space and less furniture, although it was to be some time before the Victorian stair rails were uncovered and the moulded doors stripped of their plywood overcoats. However, it was an ongoing joy to bring it slowly back to life.

We grew to love the place as a refuge. David had his own room and Kim came regularly during school holidays. We even acquired a couple of cats that came backwards and forwards from London to Ramsgate quite happily. In fact when I got their travelling box out of the storeroom in London they would walk into it without coaxing, knowing that they were going to where the air smelt of the sea and there was a garden which was much more pleasant than a litter box for those essential matters of toilette. John soon became a commonplace sight in the neighbourhood. He had his favourite pub and took long walks around the cliffs and harbour exchanging pleasantries with the locals. One such was an old rag-and-bone man by the name of Turd Cox. Where the name originated nobody remembers but it had stuck literally like his namesake to a blanket and that is what everyone called him. 'Morning, John,' he'd say as he passed by with his barrow. 'Good morning, Turd,' John would answer in his beautiful voice.

In the summer of 1969, just after *Dad's Army* had begun to gain a foothold in the public's heart, John was asked to make a film in Venice. It was one of those 60s capers called *The Midas Run*. Temptation enough, but what made the offer irresistible was that the star of the film was Fred Astaire, who had been a hero of John's since he was at Sherbourne all those years ago and he was very keen to meet him. The problem was that John was in the middle of a series of *Dad's Army*, but the film company were happy to let him work weekends only, and prepared to pick him up after TV recording on Friday evenings, fly him to Italy and deliver him back to London late on Sunday nights.

John marvelled at the luxury of the hotel in Venice to which he was whisked at sundown across the Grand Canal and said it was a far cry from the *Dad's Army* rehearsal rooms. The next couple of days' filming was happily done in the hotel and Astaire was charming and friendly from the start. Sadly, the film was a disaster due to the fact that the Swedish director was heavily under the gloomy influence of Ingmar Bergman and the film was meant to be a light comedy, so even though Ralph Richardson was also in the cast, it was doomed. When that series of *Dad's Army* ended John was able to return to Italy full-time, the location work was done in a place called Tirrenia a few miles from Pisa. Fred Astaire and John had hit it off and found that they had a great deal in common, one being the racing scene. Most evenings they had dinner together in a little café near the hotel, which had a television set in the corner on which they could watch the racing from Milan.

One evening in the car on the way back to the hotel after filming John asked Fred if he had a favourite song out of all the musicals he had made and Fred said that he did, 'After You, Who?' from *The Gay Divorce*. John told him quite truthfully that it had also been his favourite. After a pause Fred began tentatively to sing. John said that it was a moment to treasure and felt his eyes filling with tears. 'For Christ sake's, stop it, Fred,' he said, 'before I make a complete fool of myself and start blubbing.'

Towards the end of the film they spent a

day in London shooting just one scene, in which John had to drive Astaire to Buckingham Palace in a Rolls-Royce belonging to the Queen. He had to be shown how to drive the noble motor first by a professional chauffeur, then, amidst heavy traffic, John had to pick Astaire up from a location in St James's Yard and take him to the palace. Unfortunately on the slow approach to the palace Astaire was spotted by some tourists who surrounded the car banging on the windows, so John had to pull away and go round again. Eventually they had the scene in the can and the film was completed: a flop at the box-office, but a happy episode for John. I wish that I had met Fred but he and John did not stay in touch anyway. It is a sad fact of the business that affectionate bondings take place on locations where all concerned are far from home and thus lean towards a temporary companionship – but that is usually a ship that passes during the night after the last shot.

John liked me to read any new scripts offered to him first and give him an outline of the content and a view. It wasn't that I influenced any work he chose to take on, apart from going through his lines with him,

140

nothing like that. I didn't tell him how to act and he didn't tell me how to cook. But in 1970 he received a script by Dennis Potter called *Traitor* which caused the hair on the back of my neck to rise. It was so good I begged him to drop everything and read it but, to my surprise, he showed little enthusiasm for it. The truth was that it scared him: there were speeches a page long and it was a role to stretch the boldest actor. There were scenes of drunkenness, rage and despair and John said that as all television plays were ephemeral it would just mean weeks of hard slog which would be forgotten in a flash.

However, I knew that this was important work and I would not let him be lazy about it. I hurt him deeply one night while we were having dinner in a restaurant by saying that he could, if he wished, stroll through life raising his eyebrows in light comedy without anyone knowing if he could tackle anything more intense, so if he chose the easy option no one could blame him. By then I had memorized some of the script and I was forever quoting it to him. 'Oh all right then,' he said, banging his glass on the table, 'I'll bloody well do it.' From then on until the first rehearsal he studied that script non-stop and nothing else mattered. When we went to Ramsgate he shut himself away with it: he worked on the script all day and every evening I heard his lines until I knew the whole thing by heart. John was greatly affected when Freddie Joachim told him that Dennis Potter had asked specifically for him and had written the play with him in mind.

Traitor was based on the life of the spy Kim Philby and was set in Moscow after his exposure and defection. It takes place in his ugly little people's flat on a day when the world press come for an interview. By now Philby is alcoholic and paranoid, afraid that the flat is bugged. As the play unfolds he is urged to drink by the journalists and ultimately to disgrace himself. The only thing he has left to remind himself of the country he still loves is a painting by Constable. It is strong stuff and very moving.

I never saw John work so hard, but I knew instinctively that this was the crowning point of his career and, more importantly, so did he. As he prepared we spent three weeks in Ramsgate and I guarded his privacy, even discouraging contact from our families. I manned the phone, ran the house as silently as possible and kept all vexations away. He went to the first rehearsal like a man going to his execution, so nervous that he made me go with him in the taxi for moral support. After a couple of days he asked the producer Alan Bridges if I might sit in at a couple of rehearsals as I was mainly responsible for getting him to take the part. I felt extraneous and kept well out of sight. But to John it had become *our* project and he needed to talk about it at home and as usual go through the lines.

I was allowed to be at the final recording and as I watched I forgot that John was my husband as he became Kim Philby 'the traitor to his class' exiled in Russia and sinking into alcoholism and despair. I was so proud of him and I know that by biting the bullet and taking the part John had proved to himself that he could really act and that, in spite of the years of hard and steady graft, he still loved his profession as much as he had when he started out. Needless to say, after the transmission we visited a few of London's fleshpots. After an adrenaline rush like that, an early night was definitely not on the cards.

Even for the best and most celebrated actors parts like John's Philby role do not present themselves very often. My dear John counted himself lucky to have been offered that one and I think he was quietly proud to have honoured it so. He was totally realistic about his trade and was content to resume a kind of type-casting thereafter, having now proved to all who cared to notice that his range was actually broader and deeper than might have been supposed.

However, his next job was perhaps something of an anti-climax – another comedy series, *A Class by Himself*. Although perfectly well written and directed this series never achieved classic status. He started work in the late summer of 1970 and had to spend three months in Bristol on location. We rented a lovely flat, in an annexe of the Royal Spa Hotel in Clifton, a fine hotel that commanded a view of Brunel's magnificent suspension bridge across the river Avon.

John's part was that of an impoverished and eccentric peer who lived in a crumbling stately home that needed money for its upkeep. He had a chauffeur played by Peter Butterworth, a pretty niece played by Seretta Wilson who was inevitably referred to as the daughter of Sergeant Wilson in the newspapers. In one episode John's character tries to turn his house into a theme park to raise money and in the script he goes to see his old friend Henry Bath of Longleat (playing himself) for advice. Lord Bath and John played a scene together and hit it off: there was some odd similarity about them, in looks as well as personality and once we spent the day at Longleat informally with the family.

The older son, now the marquis of Bath, was and I believe remains, a very jolly post-hippy type of fellow with long hair and a prettily plaited beard. When he asked us if we'd like to see the Karma Sutra room of the house we accepted, politely I hope. He rang for the butler and we were given the grand and faintly embarrassing tour. The butler had asked me if I had a strong stomach or a nervous disposition. Well, yes and no. A gallery of pictures depicting the wonders of Eastern sensuality certainly had a certain charm but both John and I preferred to browse around other rooms hung with less erotically distinguished paintings and the awesome library at Longleat which contains, among other priceless texts, first printed editions of the Bible and Shakespeare. Glutted with wonder and beauty we made our excuses and left.

I spent as much time as possible with John in Bristol but both the flat in London and the house in Ramsgate needed me, as well as David, now in his teens. But it was always lovely to get west when I could. On one of my visits to Bristol I was able to tell John that he was one of three nominees for a BAFTA award as Best Actor for his role in *Traitor*.

The award ceremony was in March 1971 and John was still working in Bristol but the organizers of the event rang to make sure that he could attend. They said a car would be laid on to collect him and deposit him back in Bristol afterwards so that he could be ready for work the following morning. At first they quite correctly refused to tell me if he was indeed the winner so I craftily said that John was working too hard to have to face a long drive and a nerve-wracking ordeal just for the camera to record his reaction when the result was announced. At this they admitted that he was indeed the winner but swore me to secrecy.

Great excitement followed. John was delivered to the London flat in time to have a bath, a large whisky and a sandwich, change into his dinner jacket and be rushed off to the Albert Hall where we were put on a table with Lee Remick, her husband and Christopher Lee and his wife. John by this time was in a trance: he did not know that he had won although a more cocksure person would have got a clue from the fact that we were on a table near the stage. He mumbled pleasantries to the others at the table before the proceedings began but I could see how nervous he was. He always said that actors should not be given prizes, they should be grateful just for the chance to work in a wonderful profession. To the end he truly believed that he was a lucky man. This trait is reflected in his son Robin who is now regarded after years of steady dedication to his craft as a musician, as one of the best guitarists in the business. He has the same modesty and is always aware of what a fortunate fellow he is to be doing what he loves most. Like his father he has never sought showy work, preferring to know that he is respected by his peers and largely content to make his contribution as a session musician.

John remained fraught throughout the evening but I kept the secret in spite of encouraging hints from the others. Yet when his name was announced by Annette Crosbie it somehow came as almost as much a surprise to me as it did to him.

He told me later that he remembered

nothing of the short walk to the platform or anything that he said as he accepted the BAFTA award and on the night I saw nothing as my vision was misted with tears. Robin told me years later that he and Hattie were watching on TV and that Hattie had also wept. He added that she had said that she should have been there with John. He wept as he told me this. This was not just luvviness or resentment, and I did understand: Hattie's love affair with John Scofield was over by then – he had left her for someone else and broken her heart. But she wasn't exactly envious of me. It was simply that if she had never fallen in love, then I would never have come on the scene and John would have been spared all the pain of the past years. Then it would have been Hattie sitting and blinking at that table. However, as someone said, 'Life is a book, and we have to read every page'. I found myself in John's book and now he's in mine.

Much later John was driven back to Bristol, cradling his award in a bemused but quietly emotional way. He had been escorted to the back of the Albert Hall where the VIP cars were waiting for their celebrity passengers and climbed unsteadily into the nearest limousine. 'Sorry, sir,' said the driver, 'this is Princess Anne's car.' Never mind, he was returned safely to Bristol where work resumed as a jobbing actor the following day.

Due to the popularity of *Dad's Army* and *Traitor*, John was invited to appear in a series of commercials for BOAC, later to re-form as British Airways. He had to be, truthfully, simply himself – a rather vague English gentleman travelling broad and getting into a muddle over passports, tickets, luggage and the like. Of course, he was always rescued and sent on his way by the kindness and efficiency of airline staff, usually in the form of a glamorous stewardess or a helpful ticket clerk. In one of the commercials Arthur Lowe played a cabin steward in the pompous style of Captain Mainwaring. As he wheels his trolley down the aisle and serves John his drink they both do a double take. Sadly these classic little ads were only shown in Australia and New Zealand and all that remains is a photograph of Arthur and John.

He made about ten of these commercials over two years, filmed in Hong Kong and Sydney, Australia. The first year, as Freddie Joachim had recently retired, he went with his new agent, Peter Campbell, who was also a good friend who I knew would look after him well and keep his spirits up. They flew first to Hong Kong for a week's filming, then on to Australia. En route they flew over Vietnam and the pilot drew their attention to the fact that flashes of gunfire could be seen on the ground below. It was a chilling sight.

John was in Australia for two weeks although Peter, who had a large stable of actors to look after besides John, left after a few days. John missed him very much and rang me even more than usual. He was no good at being alone, odd for such a shy man. Yet it was that very quality of help-lessness which made him so perfect for those commercials.

Sunday

Darling Joanie

Have just put down the phone from talking to you, to hear your voice made me feel much nearer.

It is difficult to adjust to the constant changes of temperature, in hotel rooms etc. but I feel much better than I did this time last week, when I had a tummy upset and a feverish chill.

The whole thing is rather unbelievable and like a sort of dream. From my hotel I have a fascinating view of the harbour and all the shipping and the millions of junks inhabited by what are known as the river people who are born, live and die on their craft. They never ever leave them; the mind boggles at the sanitary arrangements, and indeed the pollution to the water, which must be quite something. A dozen red roses plus a lot of fruit was put in my room here when I arrived, it was very touching. The same thing (carnations this time) in the hotel in Sydney. People have been very kind, and I seem well liked in both places, I have had a lot of invitations to go out, but I have either been too busy or too hot and tired just wanting something in my room. In Sydney there was a lovely group playing my sort of music, I used to go up and listen to them nightly and they played anything I asked for, 'What's new' included.

The leader – Don Merrows – knew me and introduced me to his company one night, you would have loved them I know, flute, guitar, bass and drums, with don doubling on clarinet and alto sax.

151

Peter's company was invaluable and I miss him very much now he has gone.

With all this going on I find time to miss you and David and the cats and all my friends very much. I forgot to mention that his group have played at the Newport jazz festival and they have some standing in the business. I have a TV interview to do tomorrow in the hotel and later, I have to be photographed looking bemused in a rick-shaw – which shouldn't be difficult.

The Chinese in this hotel are enchanting and all look like puckered pansies when looking up at you from having knelt down to give you a drink, or a cup of coffee, they kneel down more out of natural comfort I'm glad to say rather than subservience.

Fondest love as always

John xx

He later told me that one evening in the bar while he and Peter were having a drink, there was a party at a nearby table, behaving in that way so typical of certain ex-pats: living in the past and treating the locals like something that was stuck to their shoes. One red-faced old duffer was ordering a round of drinks from one of the 'puckered pansy' waitresses, and suddenly barked at her, 'Keep still'. She had probably shifted her position slightly. This appalled John who believed that a gentleman always showed respect to a lady whatever her age or station in life. So, although shy and non-aggressive, he found himself on his feet and walking over to the old bugger's table. 'She's not a horse, you know,' he said, 'she's a human being, kindly treat her as one.' 'How dare you talk to me like that, do you know who I am, I'm Lord–.' 'Then I suggest you get back to England, sit in the House of Lords and pick up your money with all the other old fools,' said John, 'instead of making an exhibition of yourself to these nice people.'

Peter said he was shaking like a leaf when he sat down at his table but just a little pleased that he had had the balls to do it. After that the waitress called him 'god-father' as a token of respect, *and* remembered him on his next visit.

The following year he was asked to make another five commercials, all of them in Sydney this time, followed by a tour of Australia in order to promote winter holidays in England. On this occasion I was able to join him on the jaunt, but the idea of flying terrified me. True I had flown to Ibiza and had loved it once there, but I had always hated flying and spent the journeys in a state of drug- and drink-numbed terror, which took me days to recover from and the long haul to Australia was not going to be an ordeal of just a few hours, so I was truly dreading it. Peter Campbell had also arranged to go along on the trip and colluded with John to urge me not to miss such a wonderful opportunity. John was actually filming on one of the new BOAC jumbo jets at Heathrow when he hit on the idea of taking me along to see what the first-class section of the plane looked like as a sort of rehearsal for the flight proper.

I was treated very well by everyone on board – they must have been primed about my fear of flying – and was put into the care of a charming steward who calmed me somewhat by telling me that flying was the safest means of transport and showing me how very luxurious the first-class section was. We had yet to take off. Suddenly from way down the aisle where John was doing his stuff, he sent the direction that I was in his eye-line and that I must get out of sight. Feeling very embarrassed at being the centre of attention I got out my cigarettes and was just about to light up when I was yelled at by around six bystanders not to smoke on a stationary plane. So I retired to the airport lounge and smoked away in shame. I did, however, bite the bullet and agree to go on the great adventure and what a fool I would have been to give way to my fears and miss out on it. Perhaps some of my fear and panic was somehow linked with emotional associations with Tony's death in Australia. I don't know, but I got over it.

So on a cold morning towards the end of January 1972 the three of us boarded the plane, were seated in our armchair-sized berths and offered ice-cold champagne as we sailed aloft. When we had climbed to cruising altitude we were invited to the upstairs bar for cocktails and canapés. After a delicious lunch a film was shown and later after freshening up it was back upstairs for hot tasty snacks and more drink. Peter and I played Scrabble and John chatted to fellow travellers until dinner-time when the whole over-indulgence was repeated. Even for a wet wimp like me it was impossible not to be impressed or feel pampered by such treatment. Maybe it is all very routine now for business travellers and such, but back then it was a real revelation to see how comfortable air travel could be. Remember, I was a girl who had been used to every ticket being second-class. We slept soundly in due course and were all deeply, smugly sorry for anyone who wasn't fortunate enough to be us.

We broke the journey and spent two days sightseeing in Hong Kong where our hotel room commanded a view of the harbour with its sampans, floating restaurants and colour. Two days were not enough to take it all in but we tried our best and were exhausted by the time we got back on the plane for the final leg of the journey. We arrived in Sydney on a rainy morning wanting nothing more than baths and beds but were informed that there was to be a press reception at the airport.

John was feeling out of sorts and liverish. His ankles were swollen and he felt crumpled so, for once, he was a touch waspish with the Australian press people, who hadn't the finesse of their English counterparts in those days and when a reporter asked how much he was getting for the commercials he told her to mind her own business. The poor publicist who was put in charge of us had a rough time on the way to the hotel. John said that he didn't suppose Robert Morley (who was doing the same type of commercial for BOAC in America) would be expected to meet the press as soon as he got off the bloody plane. I muttered crossly, aware of the poor man's embarrassment, that he probably did, and behaved with much more grace than John had shown, too.

Much later when we got to know the people who had been assigned to look after John during the tour, the publicist told me that he had been terrified of John at first and very much in awe of him. He had been much comforted by hearing me defend him and I was subsequently put on the payroll as John's PR-cum-minder as if there was a real danger of further regrettable lapses. In fact, the whole film crew and airline staff became our friends – a great bunch of people, full of enthusiasm and with great respect for the quality of the work coming out of England in those days. *Dad's Army* was one of the most popular comedy shows in Australia at that time and wherever we went John was besieged by praise. He of course pretended to find it a bit of a bore but in truth he loved every moment.

For myself, I can't remember being happier than I was when in Australia. I had just discovered Buddhism and its simple truths had opened up a great wellspring of energy. I felt reborn so to be in a new environment and living very much in the present in this wonderful country was a constant pleasure.

We had been booked into a hotel in the middle of Sydney at first, but, through the BOAC staff that I met during the flight, I found a small hotel on Bondi Beach which had the added advantage of a small kitchen where I was able to prepare a good breakfast for John before he went off to work. I had free days to explore the city and the surrounding countryside in my new, sharpened frame of mind. I swam from the beach where the waves were so strong and powerful that on my first swim I was knocked head over heels and came up bare-arsed and red-faced with my bikini bottom around my ankles. In the evenings John, Peter and I went to the theatres. We saw a rendition of Sondheim's *A Little Night Music* and to this day it remains my favourite musical score. I still need a fix of it at least once a week. We went to a gay club one night on Bondi and had a whale of a time. The place was full of huge hairy surfers, lorry drivers and drag queens who pounced on John and Peter. 'I've never been in the presence of a filum star before,' said one elegant queen. It was all good-natured: the 'girls' were toweringly larger than life – another great night on Bondi Beach.

We stayed there for two weeks while John completed the commercials. I resisted the urge to go to the place where Tony had ended his life. That story was over: the grief and rage I had felt when he died had settled into a misty sorrow. He would never be forgotten. I had enough memories. I saw no point now in dragging out the old regrets that had been laid away and scratching at a scar that had healed over but could still be seen in the wrong light. Instead I looked at the wonders of a new land, which had such mysteries and beauty. The bird life was extraordinary and we went to a nature reserve with a huge open aviary where the birds could come and go. I'll never forget a row of cockatoos who had become quite articulate, in a way, through listening to humans. Their main refrain was 'Scratch Cocky' in a broad Australian accent as they bent their crested heads for a caress. There were green thrushes twice the size of ours and the blackbirds were blue and glossy. The parrots, for which John had a special affection, dazzled the eyes.

Every day brought some fresh wonder. I liked the sense of danger and extremes. Weather, killer spiders – everything so big, even the portions of food served in restaurants. John would order half a child's portion and it was still too much to finish. No wonder so many Australians are un-usually tall and beat us hollow at cricket and tennis most of the time.

There was a particularly enormous man called James Collier who hosted a new TV talk show called *JC at 9 o'Clock*, which seemed a touch grandiose. Anyway, John was scheduled to be his next victim – a slightly daunting prospect as the show was networked nationwide and had been hyped as being the biggest new TV draw. JC had already acquired a reputation for being amusingly blunt. To date big James had interviewed three celebrities and insulted them to within an inch of their egos. Howard Keel was greeted with 'What's it like to be a has-been then, Howard?' A famous opera star was told 'My God, you've got a big arse'. John was next in line for this dubious honour and while he was uncon-cerned I had my misgivings even though I knew that John would be himself and probably let the fellow do his worst. I managed to lay my worries aside. We were spared any further speculation about the show when we were told that it had been cancelled due to the host's rudeness. How very un-Australian.

However, to compensate for disappointing John for being spared a public roasting JC invited us to a dinner party. His house, somewhere on the outskirts of Sydney, was big, white and grand in a formal and unimaginative way. We were shown into the living room. 'No paintings or books,' observed John quietly.

Our host was a busy little man, eager for his wife or girlfriend to take us to see the pool, over which I enthused to compensate for John's lack of interest. The hostess, beautifully chic, cadaverously thin with a piled-up coiffure, was nervous, and very eager to please us and her Napoleon. Dinner was good: there were other guests, well chosen in an apparently sincere attempt to entertain John. They, too, had been slightly foxed. JC sat at the head of the table, I was on his right and John was seated among the guests opposite. JC ate nothing but smoked a lot and there were jokes and badinage. At the end of dinner when I got out a cigarette mine host lit it with a beautiful Cartier lighter, which I remarked upon. He said, 'Let's swap,' and took my disposable one and gave me the Cartier. I protested that I didn't admire it because I wanted it, but he said, 'No, I insist, I want you to have it.'

I didn't want to have it, beautiful though it was. It was a responsibility and in truth it turned out to be a bloody nuisance as it could only be refuelled at Harrods or Cartier and I dreaded leaving it somewhere. When I bequeathed it on to someone else who drooled over it at a party a few months later it was actually a relief. Anyway, over coffee that evening, JC stood up and raised a toast to John, and then said, 'John, as we didn't get to do the interview on air, let's see how we would have got on and do it here.' John paled and replied that he didn't think he would have been a very riveting subject, but if JC wanted to ask some questions he was welcome to go ahead.

Our host launched with 'Well, John Le Mesurier, we're all very fond of *Dad's Army* out here. It's made you a household name, but to be honest, getting the part of Sergeant Wilson has lifted you out of obscurity because I'd never bloody well heard of you before.'

'Oh, very good opening,' said John. 'A charm attack.' He added, 'There's no reason why you should have heard of me before, dear boy, even though I have been in this curious business for almost fifty years. I'm just a jobbing actor, not a star by any means. As a matter of fact I'd never bloody well heard of you before either, but I'm sure you must be a very important person in order to host a talk show.'

After a short silence a few of the guests broke in to say that they had seen John in hundreds of films over the years and one woman said to JC that she was amazed to hear that he had never seen John before. Peter then jumped in to suggest to our host that perhaps the reason his show was axed was that he hadn't been very good at home-work as he seemed to be unaware that John had won Best Actor at the BAFTA awards the previous year – the TV equivalent of winning an Oscar.

'With respect,' said JC, 'it was only a tele-vision play, not a film,' thus proving that he did know about it but considered it to be of little importance.

'Quite right,' nodded John. 'As I've said, I'm not a star. In fact I could never do what you have done. Tell me, are you very disappointed at not being in front of the camera any more?'

'Of course I am,' said JC, his voice rising as somehow John had taken over this interview/interrogation. 'Show me someone who wouldn't love to be in front of a camera and I'll show you a liar.'

'I wouldn't for one,' replied Peter. 'I trained as an actor but I'm much happier being an agent.'

'You're too ugly to be an actor,' answered Mr Charm.

I had been wondering if all dinner parties in Australia were like this and had just about managed to keep my trap shut, but this was too much. 'Excuse me,' I interjected 'but since when has beauty had anything to do with talent?' The room then erupted with examples of famously ugly actors and actresses, from Charles Laughton to Margaret Rutherford and the awkward moment passed.

Attempting to smooth things further I told JC that I thought he was very brave to have put himself out there in the spotlight in the first place and asked what he did before he had his show. His nervous girlfriend rushed and gushed to tell me that he was a producer and that it was he who had produced

Tony Hancock's last show in Australia.

John raised an eyebrow at me and I kept quiet but the penny had dropped and now I remembered where I had heard of this oaf and of the mutual dislike between him and Tony. Meeting him now I realized how this man must have irritated Tony from the start. Such bullying brashness, conceit and lack of finesse was guaranteed to inflame someone as sensitive as Tony, who was also having a terrible fight to stay off the bottle at the time. An evening with JC would be bound to sent a man like Tony heading for the bar. I went to the bathroom as he launched into an account of what a talentless wreck Hancock had become. Happily I was quite sober and a few good deep breaths helped to calm down my desire to tell the little Jesus what I thought of him. The apparently interminable evening came to an end at last.

Before we left JC presented John with some cufflinks. 'They are fire opals, set in eighteen carat gold. See how the links are shaped like boomerangs?' he asked. John thanked him warmly and we left with our presents. There was a long silence in the back of the car broken by John. 'Cunt,' he said quietly, and then we all laughed like drains. I never could get John to wear the cufflinks although the opals were very beautiful, red and flashy. We gave them away as well.

Two days later the tour began. We visited Brisbane, Adelaide, Perth and Canberra. In each city there would be a press call at the airport, the interest generated as much by Sergeant Wilson as by the ostensible airline-promoting purpose of the tour. John would also sing for his BOAC supper by appearing on local TV and radio. In Brisbane he was asked what England was like at this time of year (it was February). 'Oh, it's ghastly,' he replied. 'Don't go there now, wait till May or June, when the blossom is out.' I almost died every time I heard such remarks. The fact that he was supposed to be promoting winter holidays in England had slipped John's mind completely. Silently I willed him to remember how lovely the Lakes were in winter, the quiet Cotswold towns, our majestic cathedral cities with their dear little teashops. Ramsgate … anywhere. No good. He just kept harping on about how foul the British winter was and how nice it was to have escaped it for a while.

We had never known such heat. In Adelaide it was over 40°C and we thick-blooded Brits were overwhelmed by it. We blessed the air conditioning in the hotel and in the cars which we hadn't heard of in England – well, I suppose it is seldom necessary. On one occasion John had to appear as a celebrity guest on a different television talk show which also featured cabaret-type acts such a juggling magician and a contortionist. By now, due to his affection for air-conditioned comfort, he had the wit to enquire if the studio would be nicely cool. The answer was a regretful negative, but he was told there would be fans. Hearing this he implored Peter and me to stay in the comfort of our air-conditioned suite and watch it live on television while having dinner. He wanted to spare us the two-hour ordeal. 'Better that one of us suffers than all of us,' he said wryly. So after John had been whisked away, Peter and I rang room service and ordered dinner to be sent up, along with a couple of bottles of wine.

Earlier that day we had met an English actress with whom John had worked in the past. She had given up the stage after meeting an Australian lumberjack while he was on holiday in England. The change in this rather 'luvvy' woman, the type who toured with half her possessions and made her dressing-rooms into homes from home, was extreme. She was now a happy hippy, living off the land, growing her own cannabis and deeply in love with her partner, a huge bearded man who slightly resembled Rolf Harris. They lived up a mountain outside the city, had acquired a host of stray animals and, like me, were vegetarian. We had passed a pleasant few hours with them earlier that day and as a leaving present she had given me some home-grown cannabis.

Now, as we prepared to watch John's TV ordeal, I rolled a joint and happily tuned in. The host introduced John as one of the stars of *The Army Game* whose face had appeared in countless movies over the years. Then he pronounced his name wrongly. The camera passed to John who was leaning wearily against the bar of a small nightclub set with what looked like a gin and tonic in his hand. 'It rhymes with treasurer,' he said. 'What does John?' said the host smiling brightly. 'My name, dear, and I don't *think* I was in *The Army Game.*' Once again I guess I should tell or remind some readers that *The Army Game* was a very popular British TV sitcom in the early 1960s, based on NCO life in a barracks.

The host, still smiling, corrected himself

and ploughed on with a list of questions, which John answered with wan politeness. It ended with 'Have you picked up any of our colloquialisms during your stay here?' 'Rooting,' answered John. 'I hear that word a lot out here. What does it mean, dear boy?'

The host, still smiling fixedly, said, 'Well it doesn't mean planting trees, John.' Pause. 'No, I didn't think so,' he replied. 'Hot in here, isn't it? Must be over a hundred degrees, the audience are suffering already poor darlings.' The host was beginning to sweat as well and quickly introduced the first act, which was a pretty awful conjurer. By now Peter and I had started to giggle and as the evening wore on, enhanced no doubt by the dope, our laughter verged upon the hysterical. Each time the camera returned to John and our host, John was more waspish and the host although grinning maniacally, was pouring with sweat and red in the face as he tried to ward off John's asides.

'Oh, how lovely it all is,' remarked my husband laconically as act after act did their second-rate stuff. 'I've just been sitting outside this hut on the pavement. It's cooler outside than in, and the poor audience are leaving in droves. Some have fainted dead away, they're carrying them out on stretchers. In fact I might be joining them any moment now if I don't get some ice in my drink. Funny sort of bar, this.' By the time the programme drew to a close Peter and I were rolling on the floor, tears pouring down and incapable of speech. The poor presenter was a nervous wreck and John, by now fortified by several warm gin and tonics from the pretend 'bar', had a gleam in his eye and was enjoying himself. The host thanked him for coming and John finished by saying sweetly that he would also have liked to have thanked the audience for coming but sadly they had all left before the end. Should any of them be in hospital suffering from heatstroke he would love to visit them tomorrow to thank them personally. He then said that he hoped his wife and agent had managed to stay awake and would they please have a gin and tonic waiting for him – with lots of ice.

From Adelaide we went to Perth where we were guests of honour at a party on a riverboat given by a consortium of travel agents. As soon as the Fosters began to kick in they behaved like a bunch of football hooligans, playfully throwing each other about the bar and chucking beer over each other. I didn't happen to be drinking that night and sat looking at the river, occasionally asking when the boat was going to turn around. Nothing is more boring than a bunch of drunks when one is completely sober oneself. However, mustn't grumble, as they say, and whatever happened in Australia we always found something to laugh at, or marvel at. It was bliss just being in transit – every other day there were new sights and new people, you could be in a plane for hours and still be in Australia when you alighted. It took me ages to get over that wonderment – the vastness of it was almost silencing for us both.

There were, however, certainly times during the trip when an exasperated John lost, or nearly lost, his rag. He was a man, not a saint, and not able to be the ever-patient Sergeant Wilson at all times. I can only hope and suppose that his fans realized this. Being a good actor is, after all, quite a lot to do with sublimating the self and John had as many imperfections as the next man while under stress.

In Melbourne Peter left us to return to England. We missed his companionship very much as he had looked after us so well, making sure that John wasn't exploited and over-tired. But the tour was nearly over. After Melbourne we went to Canberra and then Sydney again where John had to do a few voice-overs to the ads. We had been given 3000 Australian dollars for expenses, on top of which I had been put on wages of £100 a week for keeping John in good spirits. Thus we felt a bit flush and decided to give a party at the hotel where we had first stayed and where John had stayed on his first visit to Australia. Don Merrow's group was still the resident band and over the weeks we had often popped in for a fix of good music. We invited the crew and staff who had been so kind to us, and the group, along with a few other people who had befriended us along the way. We gave them a sit-down dinner with an open menu and although this was expensive we reckoned that we had been lavishly cared for over the past few weeks and wanted to show true appreciation of a wonderful experience in Australia.

We had heard a lot about Fiji. For a start, a woman we met who worked for BOAC told us that if the world came to an end, God would scoop Fiji up in the palm of his hand and preserve it as the one place he had got right. So, as we had all this lolly and first-class tickets for anywhere we cared to stop off on the way home, we planned to return to England via Fiji and America. It had all been too magical to go directly back to England, which was still in the grip of winter. BOAC booked us into a hotel called The Fijian and we flew away from Sydney regretfully, with many fond memories and a few mixed ones.

Fiji was, and is still in the memory, the most beautiful place we had ever seen. The drive to the hotel from the airport was breathtaking. Huge trees with scarlet blossoms were everywhere and the air was fragrant with frangipani, hibiscus and a mass of other exotic plants. We arrived in the evening as the sun was setting and the sky was streaked with every shade of red. We turned a corner and there was a lake of white water lilies turned pink by the sunset, and, riding naked and bareback on horses, were three Fijian children with flowers in their hair. They waved. It remains an image of pure beauty that I hope to keep for ever. Our hotel was on the beach away from any sign of civilization, but like a Fijian village with simple rooms like thatched huts facing the sea. It was surrounded by dense forest, which housed hundreds of exotic birds who would share our breakfast as we ate on our terrace.

From Fiji we flew to LA, for both of us our first visit to the land of la-la. After the lushness of Fiji it looked like a building site, but being a couple of star-struck movie addicts we were as excited as teenagers. This was the place where my dreams were hatched, all those wonderful films that had helped me to endure the dark days of the war as I sat in the Lyric cinema with grandma watching Don Ameche, Carmen Miranda, Edward G. or Judy Garland weave a series of fantasy escape routes which helped millions of unhappy and oppressed souls to forget their troubles for a short while.

LA was much more to John's liking than Fiji had been. Fiji had been lovely but he was not really too keen on scenery and sightseeing – he quickly became glutted by beauty. He said to me once that the countryside was lovely for driving through but not for living in. In LA we went to Graumann's Chinese Theatre and spent ages looking at the hands and footprints of all the stars we had admired. I took a photograph of John crouching over Peter Seller's prints and one on the corner of Hollywood and Vine. We did every tourist thing that was on offer. One night we went to Chanson's, the restaurant where all the stars went at that time and Cubby Broccoli, who produced the James Bond films, came over to our table to say hello to John. It tickled him pink. When all our money was spent, which took about three days, we flew home.

This time there were no first-class seats as they were fully booked and we were told that our 'freebies' could be upgraded only if there were cancellations. Down in steerage or cattle class the stewardess was rude and impatient and our overdue honeymoon was over. But it had been fun and I suppose we needed a sort of decompression chamber like that crowded and uncomfortable return flight to float us back down to earth and set our feet back firmly on the ground where they belonged.

6

Peter Sellers
114 Roebuck House,
Stag Place,
London S.W.1

8th October 1974

Mr John le Mesurier,
56 Baron's Keep,
London W.14.

Dear John,

Just back from L.A. and found your very funny, sweet letter and photograph. Many people have felt the need to relieve themselves outside Graumann's Chinese Theatre. I do hope nothing was done on C. Aubrey Smith.

Had a marvellous time on *Pink Panther*. It looks as though it may be the best of the three, which would be good, as recent efforts haven't contributed a great deal to my career.

I should love to see you and have a drink. Maybe we could go to Alan Clare's new place, *The Medusa*?

I've just moved to the above address. No furniture as yet, but I do have carpets and curtains, a magnificent kitchen, fully operative loo and a comprehensive, if not extensive, wine cellar.

Love

Peter

John had sent Peter Sellers the photograph of himself squatting over his handprints outside Graumann's Chinese Theatre. He had said in his letter to Peter that he hoped it didn't look as if he was taking a dump. They had been friends every since John had worked with Peter on *I'm All Right Jack* in 1959. Peter enjoyed John's company and they shared many interests, listening to jazz being one of their favourite methods of relaxation. John had worked on the first Pink Panther film in Rome with Peter and he was on his last film, *The Awful Fate of Dr Fu Manchu* in Paris in 1980 when Peter was already dreadfully unwell. The role of Fu

Manchu was a tiring one, demanding long sessions in make-up and it was obvious to all that Peter's strength was flagging. He played two parts in the film, the other being an elderly detective called Nayland Smith, and John played the butler who guarded him and his beloved lawnmower. Their scenes together were gentle and funny and Peter always embraced him when they met on set each morning.

By then he was married to a young actress called Lynne Frederick. Things were a bit rocky and to keep her occupied Lynne had been given the title of assistant producer which seemed to involve her walking about with a clipboard, telling actors that she had seen the rushes and gushing 'Well Done' to them. She was all of twenty-eight at the time. John treated her with his customary politeness.

One evening the cast were invited to a preview of the film *Being There* which was just about to be released. It was a great evening and it was good to see Peter in a film of such quality and to be able to say genuinely how much we loved it. Sadly he died before *Fu Manchu* was edited and the American moneymen who had financed the film played up the American actors in the cast and ripped the heart out of the script so that the sense of it was lost – as were many of the lovely scenes between John and Peter. However, there had been good times in Paris while the film was being made. One pleasure was getting to know Sid Caesar – a big Hollywood star and a thoroughly nice person who, like John, enjoyed the occasional joint. John sent me this post card while travelling from Switzerland to Paris after doing some filming in the Alps.

Mont Blanc
Saint Gervais
Switzerland
Tuesday

Dearest Joanie

(The world Of Charlie Kunz – volume 3 Memories of Elsie and Doris Walters at Carnegie hall – part 1)

The above name of this particular album I came across in the hotel, depicted on the card I send you, as I write this on the way to Paris by train.

Just had a 'smoke' with Sid Ceasar.

Love
John

To explain the first lines of the card, John and Peter used to make up unlikely titles for album covers, such as 'An Evening with Arthur Mullard' or 'Rita Webb sings Gershwin'. During the journey he saw Sid Ceasar having a 'smoke' in his compartment, popped his head around the door and said, 'If that's what I think it is, give us a puff, Sid,' which surprised Sid who had got John down as a rather grand and aloof old duffer. From then on they became firm friends and on my visits to Paris, John and I would go up to his suite before dinner to share a puff or two and set the world to rights. Once he took us on a tour of the Paris subway to show us how easy it was to get about. He said that until recently he had been ferried about in limousines as nobody walks any distance LA. Paris was a whole new way of life to him and sightseeing was a great novelty. John managed to grin and bear it, not being mad about public transport, even French.

Years later when we were visiting John's son Robin in Los Angeles we got in touch with Sid again and spent the afternoon in his home. On entering, John spotted across the room a small painting by a French Impressionist. This pleased Sid who modestly showed us the rest of art collection. His lovely house, though grand, wasn't 'decored' as some Hollywood homes are. The paintings had been acquired over the years and chosen with astute passion and the house was a real home. It is hard for us English to grasp the extent of Sid Caesar's fame in the United States; in his heyday he was one of the biggest stars in America. His TV programme *Show of Shows* commanded top viewing figures nationwide and the very best scriptwriters worked under him. The guest stars were people at the peak of their careers; the film *My Favourite Year* starring Peter O'Toole was based on his show.

Sid had told us during one of our pre-dinner confession sessions in Paris that the stress of his work and his fame had given him a taste for alcohol which had got out of control, and which, to his credit he had conquered aided by the odd joint, a lot of self-control and a disciplined attitude to health. Hence our outing around Paris with John wishing he were seeing it from the inside of a comfortable car and Sid enthusiastically showing us the wonders of the Paris metro system.

Early in 1976 rehearsals began for a musical

version of *Dad's Army*, presented as a war-time variety show and cleverly conceived to include a good few of those songs which can make many of us blub, even young ones. At one point John sang 'A Nightingale Sang in Berkeley Square' which generated sufficient sniffles massively to enhance Kleenex sales every night. It was a very wistful and touching moment, a show-stopper which resulted eventually in John meeting Derek Taylor, who produced an album of songs from the show and was to become a close friend for the rest of John's life. Derek used to work closely with the Beatles and by the time John met him he was working for Warner Brothers. He put an elaborate backing track behind 'Nightingale' which John enjoyed enormously, and then asked if John would like to make an album of some of his favourite things, just for the hell of it.

It was one of the happiest times in John's life. Together they chose which songs to include and their tastes were remarkably alike. Derek gave John a book of short humorous essays by Stephen Leacock, which John knew well, many of them having been favourites of his father. So two of Leacock's non-singing pieces were included, there was some Noël Coward,

Annie Ross was asked to do a guest spot, singing 'What's New?' and Alan Clare, a favourite pianist and friend of both John and Peter Sellers, contributed a piece of his own and accompanied Annie. 'What is Going to Become of Us All?' was the title they decided upon for the record and it's a gem of an album, timeless. Derek knew that it would never be a runaway hit, but it has trickled on for years and still gives me great pleasure to listen to it and to John's half-sung, half-spoken light tenor, reminiscent of Rex Harrison's Professor Higgins in *My Fair Lady*.

The *Dad's Army* show ran at the Salisbury Theatre in London for six months before it went on the road. This was a period when our lives took on a pattern and a routine which was quite pleasant, although exuberantly sociable evenings together were difficult to arrange, particularly during the week as they either involved me picking John up from the theatre and going on somewhere, or staying home in order to feed John at a late hour. Incidentally, the Salisbury was one of the theatres which had been built by the family of John's first wife June Melville, and where originally the architect had forgotten to include dressing-rooms.

I had planned to spend the first two weeks of the tour with John in Blackpool but just as the tour began I learned to my great sorrow that one of my dearest friends, an actor called Mike Pratt, one of the stars of a cult TV series from the sixties called *Randall and Hopkirk Deceased* (revived as I write and starring Bob Mortimer and Vic Reeves) was dying of lung cancer. He had been taken to a hospital near Guildford and I wanted to be near him to help in any way I could. John understood and in his usual unselfish way ploughed on alone. He wrote me this letter from Blackpool.

Clifton Hotel
Blackpool
April 16th, 1976

Darling

I went to stay with Derek T's mother, very pleasant. I am OK and I hope you are holding out.

I think of you all very often. Much to tell you but it can wait. Unproductive morning, leave alone working.

Sat down on the bed where I had forgotten I'd left the breakfast things so wetted the bed and myself.

Felt ashamed when I had to summon the maid.

I have never seen so many ugly people all together in one place. I love you.

Had a letter from a Japanese male student in Barrow, who says he has been in love with me since leaving Japan.

It is well written and rather sad. What can I do? Perhaps Marje Proops of the *Mirror* could help.

As always,

John

And again from Manchester.

The Rembrandt Hotel
Manchester
Tuesday

Darling Joanie,

It was good to talk with you on Sunday.

The business has not been too brilliant though the houses were very good the last three nights.

The Hotel Is OK but the bedroom Is

curious. I keep bumping into things! We usually eat at the Playboy Club next door after the show, as the Hotel doesn't do any food. The Management and the Bunny's are all very kind to us. I have had the good fortune!! To have had coffee with Pat Phoenix who is going back Into 'The Street'. Johnny Mathis came up to me at Granada the other day and said nice things, so we had a drink.

He seemed very pleasant. Had supper with Anne Shelton* recently, she was here on a gig with the Milla Band, she was very pleased to see me and sends her love. She's lost five stone. Her sister was of course on hand. She seems to have lost her looks. She was very pretty as I remembered.

As I said Blackpool on Sunday was very cold and bleak, but I had a good Sunday lunch somewhere. In the evening I had a Welsh rarebit in the Midland Buttery, with Tony Brandon and old Arnold** I seem to have been away weeks.

* A statuesque and popular singer of ballads in the 1950s.

** Arnold Ridley, Godfrey in *Dad's Army* early 1960s.

Very funny letter from your Dad, which cheered me up. Very funny about Oldham and the North In general.

My dresser is coming to Ramsgate next Friday. I told her to ring you. She is very nice and bright.

The reason for her being there astounds me.

Ramsgate is the H.Q. for some society to keep *The Goons* going on and they all meet up once in a while.

She will tell you how I am perhaps better than I; Give her a moment if you have the time.

T.V. to do on Thursday. Pebble Mill or something in Birmingham.

My fondest love to you and everyone.

As always
John

During John's tour of the show Mike Pratt died. He was only forty-five and it was a terrible loss to everyone who had known and loved him. Two days before he asked me if I would go to Ramsgate and take his two children there. It was a strange request as he had been divorced from his wife, the mother of his children, for a long time. The children were quite small when they split up and they didn't know Mike very well, but oddly enough his wife agreed to send them to me, odder still they arrived on the day of his death and were in transit between our two homes when the end came.

Karen, his daughter, was fifteen years old and Guy thirteen at the time. My son David and his wife Susie picked them up at Ramsgate station and when I saw Guy it was a continuation of things past for there in my home was a young Mike just on the threshold of life, a perfect replica of my dear old friend. They stayed with me until the funeral and we all went together to see him off. I had bought them outfits for the funeral, a white Indian cotton suit for Guy and an ethnic embroidered dress for Karen. In the east white is often worn at funerals and it has always seemed to me to be more fitting somehow, particularly since I became interested in Buddhism. When Guy's mother saw him she told me she had dreamed about Mike the previous night and he had been wearing the same clothes as Guy was wearing to the funeral. Guy is now a brilliant bass player with Pink Floyd and a top session man and we have never lost touch.

John's tour ended with a stint in Brighton,

by which time he was exhausted. I spent the last few weeks of the tour with him. However while there he was involved in a Monty Python-inspired film called *Jabberwocky*, and three or four evenings a week he was whisked away after the show to a hotel near Shepperton studios to meet up with his friend Max Wall who was also in the film. John said that however late at night he arrived Max was always waiting with a drink at the ready and they would spend a pleasant hour together while John ate a light supper before retiring to bed, only to be called at an unearthly hour to begin filming.

Most of his scenes were spent in a royal box watching the Jabberwock tearing the king's knights to pieces and being covered in blood and gore. He would be delivered back to the hotel by four o'clock the next afternoon still none-too-clean after his day's filming. The fake blood was hell to get out of his scalp and I'd run him a bath and get to work on him with shampoo and the loofah. Although he complained about being over-stretched he was happiest under pressure. John suffered from outbreaks of a nervous skin condition called psoriasis for most of his life and he said that it was caused by two things, working, and not working.

Max Wall was someone else with whom he forged a close bond and they kept up a correspondence and met whenever possible. On one occasion he came to Canterbury to do a week at the Marlowe Theatre and John took me over to see the show and meet him afterwards. I found him difficult to warm to, however. He did not seem to have a way with ladies, or perhaps it was just me. I reckoned that some unfortunate past marital experiences may have soured his attitude to women. Of course, he may have disapproved of *my* past, who knows, but he and John had a special bond and that was all that mattered. These two letters express both his affection for John and that somewhat melancholy outlook that seemed so typical of him.

45 Southbrook Road
London
February 25th

Dear John

Lovely, gorgeous to hear from you my friend. I love the line quote: I think of you every now and then. Unquote, because that is typical of you.

I hope your health has improved, it is so long since we gazed at each other but is this not the profession?

The answer is yes, 'we all go different ways' it's a beautiful and well-worn phrase.

I'm glad that you were amused by my antics with Mr P [Parkinson]. My antics seem to be endless and I am frankly surprised that my idiom gains praise not only from audiences far and wide but our friends the press who have been for me, to a man – leaving out mister Shulman* who never seems to like anything or even worse, understand it, I think at times of those little boys who tear the wings off flies – alas and ah well. Someone was going to write a play for you and me, I cannot recall who, but I think we would be amiable together,

Take care John, luv to you both.

Max

* Milton Shulman, theatre critic of the London *Evening Standard*.

45 Southbrook Rd
London SE12 8LJ
March 12th

My Dear John

Just to say 'Thanks for taking part in the commemorative programme on my behalf of my 75th, gawd elp me. I also think at times about the faceless enemies we have in our profession, but who needs them with friends like you.

I too remember well our stint together in 'Jabberwocky' when we sat side by side in the Kings pavilion before we were soaked in bottled blood.

I have been watching you recently on 'The Tube' with the Dads Army gang – how short we are these days of funny men!

Take care,

God bless.

Max.

This next one was written to me on the day John died. Max must have been approached to say something about John

One of my favourite portraits of John.

John at three years old.

John in *Strife*,
by John Galsworthy,
at Croydon Rep.

Hattie Jacques, John's second wife, looking glamorous.

John with Tony Hancock in *Punch and Judy Man*.

John and me 1966 in our new home, taken not long after we were married.

John in costume for
his part in *King Arthur
and the Spaceman*.

John with Fred
Astaire. They hit it off
when they filmed
The Midas Run
together.

John as Sergeant Wilson.

The cast of *Dad's Army* in uniform.

At one of the many *Dad's Army* reunions.

Clive Dunn splashes John by the pool in Portugal.

Arthur Lowe and John in the BOAC advert – it was only shown in Australia and New Zealand and this photo is all that remains.

'I'm not usually like this. Love John' he wrote on this photo. (Don Smith, *Radio Times*)

John messing around.

John pretending to help with the gardening.

John at the piano.

and clearly braced himself to say some kind things to me as well.

45 Southbrook Road
November 15th

My dear Joan

This is to tell you that the T.V. people called too late to arrange a journey up to town in time for the bulletin.

I am sad needless to say, I was all ready to leave. It was a bad shock to me anyway, for I thought that John was a lot better by his last letter.

My deepest sympathy is with you

Sincerely

Max

In the autumn of 1976 John was offered the lead in *An Inspector Calls*, one of his favourite J.B. Priestley plays. He jumped at it without much considering the fact that it involved working in Salisbury, Rhodesia, now Harare in Zimbabwe, then in the midst of the original independence troubles. Another reason for his wanting to take on the job was that Andrew Ray was to play his son. Although a young man, Andrew was already a seasoned performer, having been cast as the lead in a British film called *The Mudlark* when he was little more than a tot. I seem to remember this involved his urchin character surprising Queen Victoria by settling himself upon her throne. Anyway, he stole the film, as they say.

He came from the same stable as John: his agent was Peter Campbell and his father, the comedian Ted Ray, had been an old friend. John, who had never visited Rhodesia, was curious to see it. The political situation didn't deter him, although after he left I had a call from an actor who had put him up for the Garrick Club in London and who was irate when he heard that John had ignored the boycott by the acting profession. The man had recently married a black actress and felt very strongly about this defection. He said that it was no use belonging to a club that he obviously wasn't going to use. If John thought about the political implications he dismissed them by saying that the arts were the bridge that should connect people, not divide them, and so undeterred he signed the contract and never did join the Garrick.

According to Andrew, John's accommodation was in a posh hotel on the out-skirts of Salisbury while the rest of the cast were in a downtown hotel, which was much more basic. It made him feel isolated and after a few days he asked to be moved in with the others. The heat made him ill – he could never bear working in hot climates – and of course the situation, being in a war zone, made the whole atmosphere unreal and uneasy. Andrew said that quite often as they sat in the hotel sharing a drink after rehearsals they could hear gunfire on the outskirts of the city.

Andrew's wife Susan was Rhodesian and lived there with their two children. They were separated but good friends neverthe-less. Andrew said that the white Rhodesians who had lived there for years still carried the same unchanging values and assumptions they or their parents had brought with them from pre-war England, and were polite and gentle, their children well-mannered and fresh-faced, most of them were apolitical, and assumed that things would remain as they were for the rest of their lives. Many had become accustomed to a far more com-fortable and prosperous lifestyle in Rho-desia than they or their forebears could ever have aspired to in Britain, and did not much fancy giving any of it up if majority rule came. Andrew said that we in England knew more about what was happening in their country than the residents did, and they couldn't understand why the rest of the world hated them.

John wrote to me upon arrival.

George Hotel
Avondale
Rhodesia
Sunday November 7th

Darling Joanie

It seems such a long time since leaving London and I'm missing you very much. However, I feel, and Andrew agrees with me, that you would have lasted out here for about five minutes such is the situation, and they way the African waiters etc are treated by the white people.

The servants in the hotel seem so lovely and gentle and smiling that I want to give a party for them all before I leave this pox ridden place, but I'm told that it would be unwise. People know me here and are nice and kind. I get asked out, but never go.

I have done interviews on radio and T.V.,

which have been well received.

I have found the part very difficult to learn this time round, but I pray I have got most of it now.

It took me 5 or 6 days to get sort of acclimatised; I felt wobbly on my feet for sometime and was inclined to nearly fall over when I was rehearsing. I am told it is due to the altitude, six thousand feet above sea level, I gather all newcomers from England suffer from it.

If Andrew wasn't here, also Isabel (from Peter's stable) I don't think I could have stood it.

I have become very close to him, and I think he to me. We manage to laugh quite frequently. I have met his wife Susan who is sweet and very pretty, their two children are enchanting, Madeline and Mark, they think I'm silly, so that's okay.

I shall be glad to get the play on now and I am already looking forward to returning … I can't stand this heat, I never go near it. Thankfully it is pissing down with rain at the moment. Glad to hear about the house and the contract, I know that you can deal with it yourself.

I love you,
John

Just after that letter, while we were negotiating the purchase of the Ramsgate house in London Road before which John and I had first kissed passionately years before, something happened to cheer him up and make the rest of the time there bearable. He met a South African woman and had an affair. She was widowed with two young children, quite well-off by the sound of things, and had a house in Salisbury and another in the mountains, with a swimming pool, where the air was cooler. She invited him there for the weekend, and in the fresher atmosphere John immediately felt better. She was quite pretty and carried a gun. He found it all very glamorous and they became lovers.

Andrew, who was privy to it all, said that she was lonely. He thought that she was looking for a more permanent relationship and John being a visiting celebrity probably seemed like quite a catch. Apparently when she saw him off at the airport she wept. It was all very romantic and when I met John at the other end he was quite emotional about it and told me everything. I believe that he was quite flattered by the interlude and had had a genuinely loving affair. It speaks well of our relationship that he could tell me all about it. Anyway, who was I to show any jealousy after the way I had behaved? He said that when they parted she had said that she couldn't bear not knowing if she would ever see him again, and he gave her his address. A few letters arrived from her, parts of which concerning her life out there he read out to me, and then they stopped. I worried a bit when I found that she was still writing to him via his agent Peter Campbell and felt that the thing was getting deeper and more serious.

One night, in spite of knowing that John loathed confrontations, I asked him if he had any future plans about his relationship with her, and if so what were they? He had been asked to do a Molière play in Perth, Australia, in a few months. Would he see her en route? Much as I could understand the attraction of an affair, I felt we had been through too much to throw away what we had rebuilt together. I loved him and our life and, unlike John, I wasn't going to give it up without being sure that it was what he really wanted.

Dear John, he was appalled at the thought of our parting, it hadn't even entered his mind. The idea of living in Rhodesia or

South Africa, or giving up our homes here and starting again was out of the question. He was much too lazy to begin again: it was simply that at the time the romance had appealed to him and now he wanted to leave it at that. When I asked him if she felt the same way, he showed me her letters and it seemed that she was hoping for much more. I pointed out that it wasn't really fair to her under the circumstances and he wrote to her saying so, thus ending it.

Years later, long after John's death and while I was doing publicity for my book *Lady Don't Fall Backwards*, named after a classic *Hancock's Half Hour* episode during which Tony sought out a book in his public library, which was missing the last page, I was in Birmingham being interviewed for a local newspaper. A young woman who also worked on the paper came up and told me that she had met John when she was very small, that he had known her mother while he was doing a play in Rhodesia. I guessed that she was the daughter of the woman he had had such a lovely time with, and by the way she was weighing me up, I knew that she was well aware of what had transpired between John and her mother. I longed to ask her lots of questions about her mother but I didn't. I did say that I believed that she had been very kind to John out there and left it at that. After all the interview I had just given was largely about my relationship with Tony Hancock so I had no right to dig into her mother's life. I would have liked to ask if she had remarried though and whether she was happy. I didn't even know her name.

Early in 1977 my son David, who by now was a talented songwriter and singer, was asked by a potential agent to audition for some record producers in the States. He and his wife Susie had been invited there by a mutual friend and the invitation included me so I took the opportunity to have another look at Tinsel Town and went along to help give him support. John was doing a publicity tour for his album, and after the launch he was due to leave for Perth, Australia, where he was to play the lead in Molière's *The Miser*. He decided that it would be better for me to join him after he had completed the rehearsal period of three weeks and be there for the opening and the run of the show (a month) so that we could travel home together. This time there was no free ticket for me, but John needed me to be there with him. He wrote this letter to me while I was out in LA, apprehensive about the play, but excited that he would be seeing his son Robin who by now was playing guitar in Rod Stewart's band and likewise touring Australia.

Barons Keep
London

Darling Joanie,

First of all I hope you are having a lovely time out there and David is getting on OK It is Saturday as I write this and I am off as you know tomorrow at 6:30. Having lunch with Peter, coming back here afterwards, when Chris will pick us up and thence to Heathrow. Suddenly the whole thing has hit me smack in the eye. I have had no time (or inclination) to study the script.

Have done 15 Radio chat shows and T.V. appearances since the launching lunch at the Savoy on January the 12th. It went very well, and the general consensus of opinion at 'Warners' and other sources said it was by far the best launch of that kind that they had organised for about six years. Lots of nice people there and to coin the cliché the

'Vibes' were very good. Derek sat on my right and Jan Francis on my left. The South's and Annie and Peter and 2 other Directors from Warners. Derek made a good speech and introduced me and I made a funny response to what he had said about me, saying, how lovely to be at the Savoy (my favourite hotel) and so much nicer than the other one, (Dorchester) and so far as I could see not an Arab in sight! (Big laugh) and then told them why it was called 'What Is Going To Become Of Us All' saying that I was leafing through some second hand albums, up some crack or passage off the Charing Cross Road, and found one called Zed Reppel in, 'The Crunch' and 'Mobile Instinct' So if albums can be called by those titles, why not 'What Is Going To Become Of Us All' what indeed? (Laugh) So it all went well and all were pleased.

I hope I have done the right thing. I am starting to pack soon, the 2 Nicks are here and I shall have an early night.

I am at the Sheraton Hotel in Perth. My Robin will be there, in the same hotel with Rod Stewart on February the 4th. I have to do some Radio and T.V. out there so I am told. Never mind!

Long to see you in Perth in three weeks time.

I love you.

John xx

With regard to the album launch at the Savoy, Clive and Cilla Dunn had also been invited and they recently told me this story about the occasion. They were sharing a table with no other than my favourite author Laurie Lee, who was in a charming state of inebriation while also flirting mildly with Cilla. At the end of the festivities Laurie Lee got up to leave and finding that he had left a large glass of green chartreuse on the table, produced an envelope from his pocket into which he poured the sticky substance, he then put it in his pocket and left.

In Australia, however, things did not go to plan, although John did get to see Robin for a couple of days on the Rod Stewart tour. I returned from LA and had spoken to John several times on the telephone from Perth. Each time he said he regretted not taking me with him from the start: he was deeply unhappy and longing for me to get out there to be with him. The heat was ferocious, it being midsummer in Australia, he didn't like the director, he hadn't connected with any of the cast members and he was feeling alone and insecure. All the confidence that winning the BAFTA should have awarded him seemed to have evaporated.

On the day I was to leave for the airport I was packed and waiting in the flat with David for the car to arrive, when the phone rang. It was Peter Campbell in a very agitated state. 'Thank God I've caught you,' he said. 'I've just heard from Australia that John has been taken to hospital. He collapsed with exhaustion during rehearsal and as soon as he is up to it he is coming home.'

'But I've got to go and get him,' I said. 'Thank God you prepared me.' The idea of another tragedy in Australia was too awful to address.

'No, you *must* stay there. He insists on coming home, you may cross in transit and it would hold him up. He's quite desperate to get back. He's off the play and his understudy has already stepped into the breach.' Shocked and frightened, I was desperate for further firm news but Peter just said that it sounded like a nervous breakdown or heat stroke. We could only guess at what had gone wrong. One moment I was waiting for a car to take me half-way around the world, the next I was waiting to find out if my husband was seriously ill or had been replaced due to professional problems. It was a nerve-racking time and I thanked God for my son's presence. Peter repeated that I should stay put and wait for news and to try not to worry, or tie up the phone.

Early the next morning I was told that John would be home in forty-eight hours, that he was resting in hospital but he would be fit enough to fly. Peter and I went to collect him from the airport two days later. I was scanning the crowds coming from the arrivals door when I heard a weak voice say, 'Hello, darling' and there he was in a wheel-chair, looking gaunt and older by many years. Somehow I had expected him to come ambling out under his own steam. And the sight of him caused me to burst into tears. Peter, capable and comforting as ever, got us home smoothly and as John entered the London flat he murmured, 'Thank God, I didn't think I would ever see you or my home again.' We got him into bed immediately where he fell into a deep sleep.

Peter told me what he knew so far, which was very little. He said that the Australian director had naturally been disappointed at John's collapse but not very sympathetic. It was the first time in his career that John had been unable to fulfil a contract and although often quoting Noël Coward's '*Why must the show go on?*' he was deeply professional.

He slept the rest of that day and all night as if in a coma. The following morning when he awoke he was able to eat a boiled egg and some bread and butter. Although his voice was weak and he had obviously lost a lot of weight he was deeply relieved and happy to be home with me and our beloved cats who were curled up on the bed as if knowing how much comfort their presence was giving him. I rang the doctor, who diagnosed depression and prescribed antidepressants. I said that I thought that John was only depressed because he was ill, to which the doctor replied that he was ill because he was depressed. Giving the doctor the benefit of the doubt, I gave John two of the pills, with the result that the following day he was semi-conscious. I threw the rest of them down the lavatory and when the effects of the initial dose had worn off we decided to get to Ramsgate as soon as possible.

By now we had bought the large detached

house in London Road, with a big, wide garden. As I have said, our new home, strangely, was the house where Sheila had stayed all those years before on the night we had become lovers. We spent most of our time there, both eager to get to its comfort and security after hectic times in London or elsewhere, and to the solid support of my parents. So I rang our favourite Ramsgate hire-car firm and our local driver came to pick us and the cats up and take us to the sea air and peace of dear ramshackle Ramsgate. As soon as we arrived I rang the family doctor who came immediately and diagnosed a serious liver problem.

The following day John was admitted to Ramsgate hospital for tests. The consultant told us that he was suffering from cirrhosis of the liver. There was no treatment, just bed rest and total abstinence from alcohol. John was told that to go on drinking would kill him. When I asked about diet I was told that he could eat anything he fancied, which made no sense to me at all, so I called in a naturopath. He was a scary little man who, after examining John, walked me round the garden and told me that unless I took his advice my husband would die quite soon. So it was raw fruit, raw vegetables, no tea or coffee and filtered water for the next two months. John complained bitterly but I had the upper hand. He lost more weight and looked awful. Friends who came to visit were shocked by his appearance, but gradually he got better. The next examination at the hospital amazed the specialist: his swollen liver had returned to normal size. Gradually I was able to introduce other more appetizing foods into his diet and his strength slowly returned.

During that awful time he and Derek Taylor began to correspond regularly. Writing and receiving letters kept John in touch with the outside world and Derek's letters were about the only thing that made him laugh. This card from Derek came with a newspaper cutting:

London April 12, 1977

A FRAIL, hard-of-hearing 85-year-old mugger, supporting himself on a walking stick, was told at the Old Bailey yesterday: 'It's time you forgot about crime.'

Well I don't know any more.

Derek

John replied:

8 London Road
Ramsgate

Dear Derek,

I seem to write a lot of letters these days. I suppose it is a sign of old age! I even wrote to the Local Newspaper about some project to disallow children to play around in some enlarged 'pen' on the East Cliff in this rather retarded town. One of the members of the Council is, as I write this, languishing in jail in Canterbury (the food in prison is better there); for having forged (nearly beautifully) some million pounds worth of Dollar Notes!

At least he had a go.

I often think about you and wonder how you all are.

If you have a moment, please let me know.

Love,

John

P.S. The Daffodils are nearly through. Over eager no doubt. Perhaps they will survive if no more holocausts occur.

Please forgive spelling and indeed hand writing.

That summer he was able to work again and appeared as Sergeant Wilson in the last series of *Dad's Army*. It was obvious from his appearance how ill he had been. I'm sure that the powers that be at the BBC thought that they had better wrap up the series before he gave the whole thing up for them. But even though the work came back slowly, it wasn't long before he was back in harness.

Dear Derek,

So here I am in glorious Leeds. It is Sunday evening as I write, and it's pissing down outside.

I have recently been re-reading some of the diaries of James Agate. I always find it nostalgic writing and a pretty fair comment on his *particular* times. As you know he was frequently saying things like – reviewed four books from 3 o'clock to 7:30. Then to the Princes Theatre on behalf of the Sunday Times, to catch a revival of 'Hedda Gabler' or something and finally ending up for supper at the Cafe Royal, where some young embryonic critic suffering from acne comes up to him and tells him his Express articles are utter *bosh*! Finally on getting home, does some revision on EGO$_4$, during which Alan Dent plays a Brandenburg Concerto on the Gramophone. And so to bed at 3:30. Next day he finds with tax and expenses etc. for all the work he has done, that he ends, with Five Shillings for himself!

I sometimes find precisely the same happening to myself. I am here to do a guest appearance on someone's programme. Top whack is £200, and getting up here, and staying in this station hotel, I will no doubt arrive back in Ramsgate with *Ten* Shillings! Another Agate entry... In another part of his diary he recalls a story about Mrs Patrick Campbell.

Terribly bored by an elderly scientist drooling away about *Ants*. 'They are wonderful little creatures, and they have their *own* police force, and their *own* army' – She leaned forward with an expression of the utmost interest, and in a voice like damson coloured velvet, said, 'No navy I suppose?'

See you one day I hope. Love to you all.

John

Then from Derek came this note in reply:

Sudbury
Suffolk
June 13, 1978

My Dear John

Thank you for your last two letters. I would ask you up here but you know you are welcome. When would you care to come? It is very green now; remarkable after such a brown and white winter. (Rivers can be *most* aggressive). I hope the budget is good for you. It is very Tory and clearly intended to bring Rod Stewart back as soon as possible. Sirs Keith and Geoffrey have missed him terribly. He was the life and soul of their dinner parties. Your letter from Leeds was strongly evocative. I have been in that hotel on that night of the week in that weather, hiding inside a bottle of gin (*never* Gilbey's) for Just such an event as drew you there, only I was on the luxurious side of the footlights and able to charge every damn thing to expenses.

Artists have always been punished and the reasons are not hard to discern.

213

During my time with the B–* I found envy was a daily visitor and malice mostly in close attendance.

Borrow 'Braine on Priestly' from the library if you can. Don't buy it – not because it isn't good, but it is too expensive for what it is. What it is is an interesting (since they have quite a lot in common, including at least two initials) but too slim volume on the development of that most prolific and wonderful man.

And, anyway, anyone who has played the Inspector in Rhodesia should read it.

You were just in time for that visit, Squire. It will help you to place current events in a familiar context. Nothing like travel for filling in details.

I don't care to fly any more. I heard a frightful description of the noises made by American forklift trucks fitting engines to DC10s, a description offered by a British engineer using words like 'grinding screeching and crunching'. All the worse when he said that the service manual for such planes forbade the use of forklift trucks anyway.

Very good Private Eye cover on the subject this week, and a wonderful cartoon of the

* Beatles

214

Pope (on page 3).

James Agate ... what wonderful reading. If only I had been born that clever or worked that hard. On balance, however, things have been rather good and I must not complain though I do so, every day and always have done. My dear Joan* has suggested I write a thoroughly grumpy play, full of nasty irritable people. Would you like to be a nasty man in it, if I can get M. Codron or M. White** to pay me £400,000 to do it? I could make you a filthy slimy pederast with a huge grog-blossomed nose and stained trousers, if you like and horrible shoes. Everyone could be crammed into a toilet in Wolverhampton Railway Station at 2 am on Sunday in January for the entire play, screaming racist filth and sexist muck at porters and passers by. It should be great fun for American tourists. Perhaps Morley could play the stationmaster who has unpleasant photographs taken in the booth on the station. It could give him a new direction

* Derek's wife

** Michael Codron and Michael White (Producers)

He has been walking through too many parts over the years though he *does* walk well. ('Walk this way please.' 'If I walk that way I'll be arrested' (laughter)).

More later Dear John. Live to Joan, or rather *love* to Joan,

From all at Number 11.

Derek

Towards the end of the summer I had a phone call from Annie Ross. Throughout John's illness she had been a regular visitor to Ramsgate and her presence did much to keep John's spirits up. She too was a member of Peter Campbell's stable and it was through Peter and with his permission that she told me some disquieting news about John. He was beginning to drink again. He had taken Peter into his confidence and then sworn him to secrecy, putting him into an awkward and unenviable situation. I knew how unhappy John was without his routine of the pre-lunch and pre-dinner drinks. I had tried to wean him on to various alcohol-free beers and Hattie was always sending non-alcoholic wines for his delectation but to

John they tasted of grape juice and nothing more.

In our local he had been a regular and popular figure, able to join in a round with the rest, but now having a double orange juice bored him rigid and was always accompanied by exhortations from his drinking friends to have a proper drink, which depressed him. Not wanting to talk about his illness, he stopped going to the pub and therefore gave up a small but pleasurable part of his life and this depressed him even more. When he was in London working, however, he lapsed and allowed himself the odd beer or small vodka.

When I heard this my first emotion was anger, less than a year had passed since he was told that he was dangerously ill and to save his life he must never drink again. He was only sixty-five and with luck he could have another twenty years, but it seemed that he didn't want them without the company of Madame Vodka or her friends Gordon and Mr Johnny Walker. The strange thing was that John never got drunk. I could count on the fingers of one hand the times I could see that he'd exceeded his meagre limit, and then only I would have noticed.

He abhorred drunkenness in people, especially women, thinking that it demeaned them particularly, and yet he was prepared to risk his life for a habit that hardly seemed to change his slant on life one iota. It was a side of John's character that I never understood. I tried everything to get him to stop. I wept, I pleaded, threatened to divorce him on the grounds that I couldn't bear to watch him doing something that would take him away from me. But for all his gentleness John was stubborn.

We called a family conference with Peter in attendance. I pleaded my case, then John pleaded his, he argued that it was *his* life we were discussing after all. It had been good one, he said, up until this past year but without the pleasure of meeting friends such as Jeffrey Bernard and having a drink in the surroundings he loved, the Soho pubs like the Coach and Horses, Gerry's Club, Ronnie Scott's, the local in Ramsgate, in fact *any* pub, then a large slice of his life was missing. If he could not go into a bar and have a drink on an equal footing with his mates then he'd rather be dead. As simple as that. He said that he'd always preferred quality to quantity and that without the routine he loved he was not prepared to go

218

on. Finally he promised to drink nothing but beer and Guinness and to do that moderately, but he could not give up alcohol completely. I was out-voted and I gave up. All I could do was to treasure each day with him from then on.

The funny or ironic thing was that as soon as beer was back on the diet, he began to put on weight, the colour came back to his face, he was happy, and work began to flow his way again. He made a TV play called *Flint* by David Mercer in which he played a randy old vicar who rode around in leathers on a motorbike. (Did I say that he never got on a motorbike again after his army days? Well this was the exception.) He also got up to no good with Beryl Reid, Julie Covington and the odd choirboy. It was quite unlike anything he had done before and he loved it. The reviews were mixed – some critics liked it others were disgusted by or perhaps merely dismayed to see the noble John growing old disgracefully in a part. Do they not realize that actors *act* – that's their job, and it can be fun to play against character at times? The BBC was bombarded with letters applauding their courage in putting it on and as many voicing their outrage.

This one gave John great amusement.

Cheltenham, Glos.
23/1/78

'Letters'
Daily Express
Fleet Street
London EC4P 4JJ

Dear Sirs,

I read, with regularity, the views of your TV critic, Mr James Thomas, in his article entitled 'Last Night's Viewing'.

On Sunday, January 15th, on BBC 1, we noted in our TV programme that the 'Play of the Month' called 'FLINT' was a comedy concerning a village parson (to be played by Mr John Le Mesurier) and his eccentricities. With such an actor and such a theme, this seemed likely to be good family viewing to which we looked forward.

Whilst praising Mr Le Mesurier's performance, Mr James Thomas made no mention of the incredible filth, obscenity and blasphemy with which the play opened and doubtless continued, but we turned off the set after 15 minutes – which time was packed with innuendoes – of what was described as the vicar's 'Fuddles' with his paralysed wife's sister (played by Miss Beryl Reid), carryings on with the choir boys in the vestry and the presentation of an unmentionable item to a nunnery, which last would have taken a soldier into court for obscenity of speech, if in public.

We left the parson sitting on the bed of a lightly clad lady replacing, it appeared, his sister-in-law, now too old to attract his 'Fuddles', in or out of the vestry!

It is all very well to be given the stock reply that 'You can always turn off a distasteful programme' but surely this should not be so frequently necessary as of late.

I am surprised that a fine actor such as Mr John Le Mesurier should sully his reputation by accepting such a role, and this goes for Miss Beryl Reid as well.

This is the general opinion of many friends, not only that of my family and myself.

Yours faithfully,

Cc: Producer, Play of the Month
Mr John Le Mesurier, c/o BBC
The editor, Radio Times

Well you can't please everybody.

In the summer of 1978 John was asked to be in a Disney cod-Camelot film called *The Spaceman and King Arthur*, starring Kenneth More. It was filmed mostly at Alnwick Castle in Northumberland, on one of the most beautiful stretches of the British coast. The cast and the crew were billeted at the Holiday Inn in Newcastle but after a few days John and Kenny tired of the drive to and from Alnwick and found a hotel in the exquisite shambling village. The White Swan was hard by the castle, close to the coat where on clear days Lindisfarne could be seen and from whence they could walk to work. John sent me these letters:

Alnwick
Northumberland
July 13th, 1978

Dearest Joanie,

Moved from the Holiday Inn (for which much thanks) I am now at the 'white Swan' Alnwick.

Dear little town and can walk to work, but don't! Kenny is here too and is looking forward to meeting you, as indeed am I.

With love,

John

Alnwick
Northumberland
Monday, July 31st 1978

Dearest Joanie

More rain and we are on stand by. Spoke to Jo on the phone last night. She tells me Robin spends Sundays with Britt Eckland, the other day she brought Raquel Welsh to hear them play a gig somewhere in the canyon where they live.

Great excitement amongst the young gentlemen! Would you send a card to me with his address please?

Fond love

John

John and Kenny were impressed by Mr Disney's generosity. He paid well and his largesse included letting the cast and crew charge their hotel bills including meals to the film expenses. Sadly the food at the White Swan was pretty dire. Brown Windsor soup, roast meat and trifle were offered constantly with a speciality of the day causing great hilarity between John and Kenny by its monotonous awfulness. They therefore set out to find restaurants in the surrounding area offering more palatable fare with some equally disastrous results.

A letter from Kenny's agent confirms that the area, though picturesque, had very little to titillate the gourmet:

25th July 1978

John Le Mesurier, Esq.
The White Swan hotel,
Alnwick,
Northumberland

Dear John,

I felt I must write on behalf of us both to thank you for your bounteous hospitality at the Victoria hotel, Banborough on Sunday.

Obviously in my line of business I get taken to many of the top restaurants in London by stars of stage, screen and, in case of Normal Shelley, radio; but I can seldom if ever recall a meal of such singular and unforgettable quality as the one we shared with you on Sunday. I had no idea that anyone in the professional catering industry could do what the chef at the Victoria Hotel did to my haddock:

A very remarkable achievement and one which I shall not easily forget.

We are both very envious of the rare gift which you and your friend Kenneth More undoubtedly possess of being able to seek out those unusual eating places, off the beaten track and full of local colour:

A gift enjoyed by few but the most seasoned of world travellers.

Our sincere thanks for a memorable experience.

Yours,

Victoria & Michael xx

When I went up for a visit Mr Disney's generosity embraced me as well. A first-class ticket was sent and when I arrived at Newcastle a car was waiting to take me to Alnwick. On the train from London as I passed through the carriages on my way to the dining car, I saw the Archbishop of Canterbury, Dr Robert Runcie, sitting in a crowded open compartment, and I remember being terribly impressed by his humility and rather ashamed of myself for being so grand and decadent.

Kenny More was an absolute charmer. Not for nothing had he become Britain's favourite post-war matinée idol and film star. I don't think he was ever rated in the States, or anywhere else in the world for that matter, but his utterly convincing portrayals of decent, humorous chaps in classic films like *Genevieve* and *Reach for the Sky* – in which he played the heroic RAF pilot Douglas Bader who continued to fly even after both legs had been amputated after action – were hugely affecting and popular. I felt immediately at home and at ease in his company. On location he and John shared a caravan where I used to hang out with them during filming. At John's request I had brought a few joints up with me to keep him happy. One evening after filming the three of us were sitting peacefully outside the caravan enjoying the late sunshine and John had just lit up when we were approached by some fans, a mother and her two daughters who were also staying at the White Swan.

The previous evening they had come over to our table and asked for John and Kenny's autographs. Now here they were on location asking if they might have a photograph taken with them, so I took a photo of the ladies with King Arthur and his knight Sir Gawain smoking a reefer, which Kenny thought was very funny. How shocked the ladies would have been had they known. Mr Disney, who didn't approve of such things, would probably have had John thrown off the film in disgrace.

I spent a very happy week in Alnwick and was sad to leave; meeting Kenneth was a big treat and it was nice to see how he and John kept each other company. I have a photo somewhere of Kenny and me taken by John. Kenny is standing behind me and we are both laughing because he had just said to John, 'For God's sake stop fumbling about with the camera and take the picture, Johnny, I'm getting a hard on.' I didn't see Kenny again; John met up with him a couple of times in London. It was a long stint on the film and they were both tired when it came to an end. But John always remembered that summer in a kind of crazy Camelot with great pleasure, not that I was playing Guinevere...

Alnwick
Northumberland
August 11th 1978

Dearest Joanie,

Hope you had a nice time in London. May have to see some gifted buffoon of an American director in London next week, who is doing 'Dracula' with L. Olivier. We press on slowly and the sands don't seem to be running out.

I get a bit homesick and long to see you and HIM,* in that order!

Fondest love to you and Mark if he is still there.

Love John

The film, I believe, was called *Sherlock Holmes's Younger Brother* and the 'gifted buffoon' of an American director was Gene Wilder whom John liked immensely. He had a wonderful scene where, as a high-ranking

* Nicky the beloved cat

228

but nervous officer wearing dress uniform and a plumed hat, he was summoned to the presence of Queen Victoria with a prepared speech which he was frantically rehearsing as he approached the throne. It came out as 'It would give me great pleasure to be inside your Majesty.'

He must have written to Kenny as well because I found this card from him among John's things:

Dearest John

Thanks for that immortal post card, the white swan will ever black my memory, especially that 'orrible manager!' No, you're very wise to take that film, I was sorely tempted, but they didn't come thru with enough scratch to satisfy my agent, and I didn't feel sure enough to over rule him.

Good luck, and keep me informed.

Yours till the white swan flies south.

Kenny

7

One of John's most regular – and amusing – correspondents was Derek Taylor. After working with John on the album, Derek returned to LA as head of Warner Brothers. In his brilliant and varied career he had begun as the northern show business correspondent for the *Daily Express*, and in May 1963 had covered the first Beatles concert; he was so impressed by their talent and originality that one year later he became their press officer and was ghost writer of their manager Brian Epstein's book *A Cellar Full of Noise*. Later when he left for America and set up his own publicity company his clients included the Byrds, The Beach Boys, and Captain Beefheart. He came back to England to launch Apple for the Beatles and was their head of communications. He was a close friend of George Harrison and remained so until he died in 1997. He produced some wonderful albums including among others *A Little Touch of Schmilsson in the Night* and had a warm friendship with the late Harry Nilsson. He was a rare person and remained an English gentleman for all the best reasons while also being an influential part of the flower power culture of the late 60s. He was nicknamed by the Beatles and Brian Epstein the Aristocrat of PRS, and was beloved by the Beatles, and indeed by anyone who knew him. What good fortune for John to have him produce his album, 'What's Going To Become Of Us All', just for the hell of it.

During Derek's last stint in LA he and John kept up a regular correspondence. Derek had moved his family out there lock, stock and barrel. His wife Joan and their six children intended this to be a permanent arrangement but very quickly things began to go wrong and his essential Englishness drew them home again. His joy at being back in England is evident from this letter written soon after their return.

Holly Cross Farm
Bramley
Hampshire
November 8, 1978

My Dear John

Just think, ten years ago we had never heard

231

of Dr David Owen, Larry Grayson, Roddy Llewellyn, Elton John, *It Ain't Half Hot, Mum*, Uri Geller or Moss Evan's. The only tabloid Daily was the *Mirror*, (wrong – *The Daily Sketch*, what a wonderful newspaper, still with us) and there was still a Beatles.

Was it a better world? No. Was it a better autumn? No. Why am I going on like this? I don't know. I have spent all morning writing letters on this new typewriter. I am ready to be silly, and I thought I would write to a few friends.

We move to Suffolk at the end of this month. Did I tell you? To Sudbury. I am having a P.O. Box for practically all purposes so that nearly all the mail is pleasant (and to keep Americans from my door) but for you and like-person's the address is– We are overwhelmed with relief at coming 'home' so completely – Joan and I had always wanted to live in a Constable painting, and this house is on (and over) The Stour, built as a mill 1000 years ago and converted properly some time just after the war (not the one my father called Our war, the last one) – we are very fortunate–

Los Angeles is a grim, battered memory. The three eldest children were in horrendous danger, but are now safe here and the three youngest escaped completely. This *is* without question, the country to live in, bread rationing notwithstanding and maybe because of it. I do think asking for' 30 loaves is too much. Did you read that? And one rounds man was fired at and missed, by an angry householder with an air rifle. Where, in Suffolk, are you from? My estate agent, Harold C. Percival (*very* Rotarian and rather nice) named you as a Suffolk man, while the local headmaster said that Douglas Fairbanks Jnr comes to Sudbury twice annually. So that should help, somehow. I think it is possibly time now for him to drop the Jnr, likewise Sammy Davies. Which brings me, logically, to Bruce Forsyth (who comes from Edmonton and not in Alberta) who is having an awful hammering in the press. Poor Bruce. He had it coming, I fear. Too popular. Hardly anyone escapes. Tommy Handley died in time to avoid it. Bit much, having to die so that someone like Merton Taylor doesn't kick you in the spine. Well, he'll nae kick anyone again himself. Our dear friends from M Python should be about due for a kicking. They have made a film called *The Life of Brian* which is not a million miles from the life of Our Lord. It is not nasty, but it is close enough to warrant a lot of holier than thou Squire, from Grubstreet scribblers who never give Jesus a moments thought from one Christmas Day to another large brandy please. Anyway, I am glad you have made a film for Walter Disney. It seemed to last a long time and I am presuming that you were paid throughout (I hope so) and that the delays were due to weather.

I like it up there by the wall. I was in the army in Carlisle for some time and developed a great fondness for border people and also state beer, now no more.

I enjoyed *The Lost Boys* very much and wonder whether you saw it. Ian Holm wonderful as JMB and the whole thing rekindled an interest in Barrie.

I have been haunting second hand book shops and picked up some decent 1st editions of this and that, including one book of his letters. Very nice kindly letters, but not sentimental. A good sense of irony. A friend of ours (Mary Peach) said he wrote 'some bloody awful plays' and I dare say she is right. I haven't written any at all so I hesitate to make such judgements. I have just heard the news and a baker's van has run over someone's foot.

My goodness. Is this *still* England? I had

better close before this letter is out of date and we decide to go and live in Brittany. Is there no peace anywhere? No.

Just think, twenty years ago we had never heard of The Beatles, Christine Keeler, Ian Lavender, Anthea Forsyth, Noel Edmunds, Rod Stewart, *Dad's Army*, Melvin Bragg, but we were *very* aware of Prince Charles, Archbishop Makarios, Harold Macmillan, Selwyn Lloyd and Russ Conway. What a strange world it is and was.

You know that men now living knew Thomas Hardy who was at the funeral of Palmerston who was born in 1784. It follows that there will be men living when the century turns who can throw a line back about seven removes from Shakespeare. For more information on this, please write me.

I don't believe The Queen should be encouraged to wear glasses for the Christmas address. Can you get word through please, and let me know the response.

I think the recent affair in the House of Lords set the monarch back quite a long way. I have been hearing many complaints, but it is not my business, really. I am just a commoner, yet not as common as some, or so I would think.

Thank you for the wonderful piece you

wrote out regarding the Irish Hamlet. I have it safely and don't recall acknowledging it. Must close now. Have rambled enough. The little ones are due home from the village school so I shall post all my mail and meet them.

Very best, as ever and I now have a phone: Bramley ✶✶✶✶✶✶.

To all of you, family and friend

Derek

John replied:

London Road
Ramsgate

Dear Derek,

I was really pleased to hear from you this morning, you seemed relaxed and more than pleased to be shot of memories of 'The Strip' and happenings at the corner of 'Hollywood and Vine'.

Have they managed to get the second 'O' in Hollywood straightened out yet?

It seems to make the invitation to visit there more drab than necessary. As for

'Warner Bros.', only Davis, Bogard and Groucho's correspondence, put them in the right perspective

It must have been a kind of a nightmare for you all.

Anyway the Constable Country is beautiful and you will find some peace there. I used to know it well and have fond memories of Long Melford (quite a good restaurant there now I believe), Dedham where Alfred Munnings used to live and paint his horses, also a place called Witham, where once I made a few runs at Cricket. A lovely ground as I recall and owned all those years ago by a certain Claude de Crespigny. He achieved some fame when I was at school at Sherborne, by climbing up the Abbey Tower and altering the clock by some 20 minutes in our favour. I remember all the boys had to parade in the quadrangle in shorts. So that the authorities could see which of us boys had scarred knees! *Nobody* was discovered as Master de Crespigny had the wit to flee the town of Sherborne, let alone the County of Dorset.

I am really pleased you are all back in England.

Although we don't meet often, I like to know you are *here*. One day I shall come to

Sudbury or Long Melford and perhaps we can walk about a bit and have a laugh and a joke.

In the meantime Joan and Annie Ross (who has been staying with us) send love and so do I.

John

P.S. What kind of Job are you going to take up next?

P.P.S. Have you read a book called *The Fan* By Bob Randall? Worth a go. In paperback and published by Magnum Books.

In the autumn of 1979 John began rehearsals for the Alan Ayckbourn play *Bedroom Farce*, pleased by the prospect of going back into the theatre and even more pleased by the fact that he would be on stage in Hong Kong, Singapore and Kuala Lumpur. It was put on by the Hilton hotel chain in the Far East and was presented as something called a dinner show. The idea was that the audience would wine and dine for two hours beforehand and then watch the show over their coffee and liqueurs. John, pessimistic as ever, prophesied that by then the audience would be too pissed to sit quietly and watch a play and visualized lots of ex-pat hooray Henrys throwing bread rolls at the cast, but his fears were groundless.

We left England on a freezing January day at our second attempt. Two days earlier we had assembled at Heathrow in a snowstorm, eager to be gone but only to be told that most of the snow ploughs were out of commission and the runways could not be cleared. Good old England, we always view extreme weather with surprise and are hardly ever prepared for it, be it heat wave, hurricane or blizzard, everything grinds to a halt. But eventually we were lifted up through the dark clouds and off to the clear skies over Hong Kong.

The cast were a jolly lot. John was partnered by Moira Fraser, a witty and elegant actress who played his wife and the others who I hadn't met before were all distinguished by being well-known in either popular TV soaps or serials. One, Del Henny a gorgeous hunk of a man and a fine actor, became a special mate. Very left-wing and working-class, he had lots of anger against injustice and on one occasion when we were all invited as guests to a meeting at the royal racetrack in the privileged members' enclosure and given lavish hospitality there was a nasty moment. A Lady Someone-or-Other was talking to John and seeing that his glass was empty she clapped her hands imperiously and loudly called to an ancient wizened waiter, 'Boy, bring master a drink.' John's eyebrows went up warningly as he watched Del and me struggling to keep quiet and walk away.

We were besieged by invitations. The expats regarded John as a social feather in the cap and there was hardly a day when we weren't invited, all of us, to luncheon in some richly appointed home or luxury yacht. To be honest, most of the hosts were deadly dull dinosaurs, embalmed in a world that had moved on from their dubious standards and ideas about privilege, leaving them hanging on to their illusions and each other.

However, some lovely moments did shine out. One was meeting some musicians who were appearing as a classical trio in a wonderful play called *The Lunatic, the Lover and the Poet*, starring Derek Jacobi, Isla Blair and Timothy West. We were invited to a matinée, loved it so much that we blubbed noisily and when afterwards Derek Jacobi opened his dressing-room door to us, both John and I were awash with tears. Derek embraced us both and confessed to weeping deeply himself after every curtain. And no wonder as the play is about Byron and ends with the poem 'So we'll go no more a-roving', which is already a complete tearjerker.

We also had the good fortune to meet Laurence Olivier's son Tarquin who was a really delightful and modest fellow. Over the weeks we were in Hong Kong we saw a lot of him. He seemed lonely and starved of company of the thespian kind. He saw the show more than once and each time he came to the Hilton we would lure him up to our suite where we kept room service busy bringing up snacks and drinks.

Tarquin's childhood was spent among giants of the arts. John asked him once why he had not been tempted into the theatre, which he patently adored and he replied that he had been daunted by excellence. He was a classical pianist of some distinction, we were told by others, but in his youth the world's very greatest pianists and composers were regular guests and companions of his father so he put his talent away untried. The best is the enemy of the good, as Voltaire said... He told us that he once wrote a book about his search for spirituality and his travels around India and foolishly asked Noël Coward, his godfather, to give him an opinion of his writing. Coward airily waved it away saying, 'My dear boy, nobody would be slightly interested in your soul.' He was not complaining about his lot but gave the impression of a life unfulfilled. He had chosen to be a banker, dealing in international money exchange and was obviously clever. He would say after a few scotches, 'I must be boring you to tears with all my memories,' and we would assure him in unison that it was not so. We were fascinated by them of course. He had adored his stepmother, Vivien Leigh, for her beauty and actually for her feyness. The drama surrounding her marriage to his father must have been like a fairy story to a young boy.

Once on a Sunday night when John had a night off Tarquin invited us to dinner at his house in Repulse Bay. There were three other guests, an elderly ex-patriot couple and their rather shy daughter. Dinner was a very formal affair and rather like being in a time warp. He had asked his housekeeper to prepare pheasant as a gesture to John who loved it. It was clearly massively overcooked by the way everyone was struggling with it and I thanked heaven that I did not eat game. John was in the middle of assuring his host that it was delicious when the blade of his knife snapped in half and the pheasant flew clean across the table. Making a belated bid for freedom perhaps?

We went from Hong Kong to the so-called enlightened dictatorship of Singapore, which I hated. It was so clinical and menacing. On the very first morning as we left the hotel John put his cigarette out on the pavement and in seconds a policeman had cautioned him. There were headlines day after day about the flogging or execution of 'drug addicts' who had been caught merely smoking pot. On one occasion the whole cast went to Bogie Street, which was the last outpost of decadence and where one could have drinks at sidewalk bars and watch the transvestites parade in their finery. John and I had gone on in the first taxi with company members Jennifer Wilson and Patricia Brake and as we alighted at the dark end of the street John was pounced on by half a dozen shrill drag queens who went through his pockets like a plague of locusts. Happily Del Henny who had just arrived behind us saw them off with a few well-aimed blows but it spoiled the evening and took away the gaiety for us.

On to Kuala Lumpur for another sell-out, and then home. It had mostly been lovely and luxurious. The hotel suites we were given in all three venues were sumptuous and we had once more escaped a cold winter at home. Financially it was a disaster, the bar bills from our over-generous entertaining took a big slice from the fairly modest wages, leaving us with very little. We regarded it as a holiday and nothing more, and as such it was one we would never have been able to afford at that standard. We were happy to be home in Ramsgate. Our garden was stocked with spring flowers and the cats who my parents looked after in our absence were happy to see us back. John marked the return to reality with a slightly irritable correspondence with his accountant.

8 London Road
Ramsgate
5th Feb

Dear Richard.

Could someone deal with this please? Joan rang you recently regarding continuing to send 50% of my earnings. Can it possibly be reduced?

You sent a form for me to sign regarding V.A.T., which I have sent off to you, in the letter accompanying *this* form.

Regarding our request truly, my dear fellow, are you working for the government, or me, do you bend *anything* ever so slightly?

Let's be quite honest, because I know, and you know that it can be done.

A lady for instance living in The Savoy Hotel left you for this very reason!

Come on now; let us not be more beaurocratic than is entirely essential.

Have a nice time in Sunningdale,

Love

John Le Mesurier

BakerRooke
Chartered Accountants

John Le Mesurier
8 London Rd
Ramsgate,
Kent

Dear John,

Many thanks for your note of the 5th – it

was a joy to read a more amusing letter than those usually dealing with tax matters.

I am grateful to you for your help albeit that it is not going to materially assist the tax bills.

All the best wishes to you both

Yours

Richard

John resumed his peaceful routine, reading or letter-writing in his room, which overlooked the garden. His desk fitted into the dormer window and as I beavered away at my vegetable plot at the bottom of the garden I would look up and see him absorbed in his tasks. He was completely uninterested in the garden and sometimes apologized when he saw me shovelling compost or digging my furrows, always seeking assurance that I really did not mind doing something he considered so ghastly. He need not have fretted. As with my father, gardening had become a passion for me and Dad taught me everything he knew. I especially loved growing vegetables – being able to dig up potatoes and then cook them using my own mint. I grew carrots, peas, parsnips, broad beans, spinach, sweet corn, runner and French beans, herbs ... you name it. I had hands like a stevedore, as I hated wearing gloves.

John, on warm days, would sit on the patio in a big peacock chair learning his lines while I puffed and sweated miles away in a world of my own. Occasionally he would call out 'Darling, could you bear to make me a cup of tea?' and in spite of my muddy wellies and hands I would trudge up the garden in order to attend to his needs, knowing that even the smallest domestic task was abhorrent to him. Once when I was in bed with flu and asked him to make tea, he listened carefully to my instructions, then put two tea bags in the electric kettle and brought me a cup of the foulest brew imaginable as this seemed more logical to him than the complicated method of warming the pot and taking the teapot to the kettle.

In the spring of 1980, John opened in a play at the Lyric Theatre, Hammersmith, a revival of *Hay Fever* by Noël Coward and his leading lady was Glynis Johns. In the same week at the Charing Cross Hospital just round the corner my daughter-without-law, Susie, (David and she never got around to

making it legal) gave birth to *my* leading
lady, Emma Bryony, my first and only
grandchild and the light of my life. John sent
a telegram to Susie saying, 'It seems we've
both opened in Hammersmith at the same
time.' He sauntered in to see her and said he
was pleased that the baby had just the one
head and the required number of limbs. He
sometimes said terrible, tactless things like
that to hide his emotions. Emma is Aries
like him and apparently Arians make their
presence felt and there were clashes from
time to time over the next few years. She
called him Bod after a children's TV
programme in which he did the voice-over.
'Stop it, Bod,' she would say if he pretended
to take food from the tray of her high chair,
but all in all they got on fine.

His leading lady in *Hay Fever* did not fare
so well. As soon as rehearsals began it
became clear that their modus operandi
were at odds. John always *had* to go to any
first rehearsals word-perfect, looking laid-
back and casual although he was churning
with terrors inside, whereas Glynis was a
more nervous and demanding actor who
needed lots of attention and careful
handling. It had boded ill when, even before
rehearsals began, she rang me daily asking

questions about John's personality, likes and dislikes, sense of humour and routine. The calls would take ages and as they got more deeply into the play it was obvious that he was a complete enigma to her and she became more and more perplexed by his apparent vagueness, asking me why he had done this or that or made such and such a comment. She could not grasp his humour at all and I think that was part of the trouble.

John, even though he adored women for their warmth and maternal qualities, was not one to dance attendance on this rather intrusive and demanding prima donna, and even at the other end of the phone in Ramsgate I could see how tiresome the situation was becoming as it was driving me slightly bonkers as well. By the time I went to see the play in Brighton much later when it was touring, things had calmed down, they worked well enough onstage and off they were polite but distant. Her phone calls to me had ceased by then and when I did meet her in the flesh it was very fleetingly as if we had never had contact before. She had learnt the simple truth that John was unable and unwilling to change the way he was for one second and so she just had to get on and cope as best she could because the mountain simply could not take one step towards Mohammed.

This is not to say that he hadn't admired her work for years; indeed, one of his favourite songs was 'Send in the Clowns' sung as only she could. It was a shame that they couldn't have become pals but one can't expect everyone to get on. However he did have a letter about the play from Dame Flora Robson which cheered him up no end.

Brighton

Dear Mr Le Mesurier,

Six of us came to the play during the first week – we all loved it, very funny and sometimes most touching. I thought you might not have seen this cutting which was sent to me by an American friend, it is perhaps something you all know, that the Queen loves you, but nice to see it in print.
  Long may you run

Yours sincerely,

Flora Robson

The cutting, sadly, is lost but I think it basically said that *Dad's Army* was the favourite sitcom of the royal family.

During 1980 we rented a house in Shepherd's Bush for the times that John needed to be in London. During that summer John's eldest son Robin had married. By now he had settled in LA having fallen in love with the place as well as his beautiful bride who, just to complicate matters, was also called Robin. Even odder was the fact that she had a sister called Kim. No, they never met, it would have been too confusing. By now Robin was playing guitar with Rod Stewart's band and was to continue to do so for many years. His brother, Kim, always known to everyone except his parents as Jake, was also a musician of some note. He played drums with many top bands and was in great demand for session work in studios. He was also a brilliant sound and lighting engineer and had worked with Peter Cook and Dudley Moore in the south of France setting up the equipment for a stage show. He said that it was one of the craziest and happiest times of his life.

Jake was still living at Eardley Crescent and had taken over the huge basement flat, which was always thronged with friends, some good ones, some parasites. Hattie lived on the first floor, leaving the ground floor free to swallow the noise levels, and occasionally put up visiting friends. She would phone down on the extension to enquire how many people were downstairs and, however many there were, they would be duly fed and watered. Yes, she was taken for granted by her younger son, but he had known no other way of life and had no yardstick by which to measure other mothers. Frankly, where he was concerned, I was a pushover myself. Jake was loveable; it wasn't charm exactly, that would have seemed contrived and he had no conscious charisma, but he was funny and bright, highly talented and irresistible.

John Scofield had now long departed and Hattie's heart, oversized in proportion with the rest of her, had broken, never to be mended. She worked ceaselessly on her career and with her charities, still surrounded by her friends, still giving magnificent Christmases and kindnesses but the sparkle had gone. It was this quality that her son Jake had in abundance – a mischievous, daring quality that had faded in her somewhat as if one of the lights that made her so iridescent had gone out, like one or two lights in a chandelier. Things looked the same but slightly dimmer.

On 6 October 1980 John and I were at our rented house in Shepherd's Bush, near the theatre and had just finished a late breakfast when the phone rang. John answered it. I wasn't paying much attention, probably reading the paper, but I noticed it had gone quiet. 'Yes, come over now, darling,' he said and hung up. When I looked up he was sitting staring at the table. 'Jo's dead,' he said. 'Kim found her this morning. She died in her sleep some time last night, Martin's there taking care of things.' Martin was a rather forbidding gay man who over the past two or three years had become a sort of secretary and companion to Hattie. He was very efficient and accomplished; I think he was a window dresser or had been and I know he was very supportive and even rather possessive of her. Her other friends, especially the gay ones, did not like him as he was lacking in any sort of frivolity although I'm sure he was a practical and sensible chap. I was grateful that he was there at that moment and I knew that he must be distraught at losing Hattie.

I rang him immediately and could tell he had been weeping, but he was in control and doing what had to be done. He was waiting for the undertaker and said that Kim was on his way to us. He arrived soon afterwards, white-faced and dry-eyed. What can you say to ease the pain of such a loss as this? I faded into the background and left the two men to their sorrow while I made coffee and tried to be useful. It was a ghastly day. John had to ring Robin in America and break the terrible news. Then he called Hattie's brother, another Robin, and then the friends before they heard it on the TV or radio.

Joan Sims was inconsolable; Hattie had meant more to her than anyone, she was liked a sister and mother all rolled into one. I do not believe she had any close family, her mother was dead and she was an only child. It speaks well of Kim that he drove over to her flat and brought her to be with us. We stayed together all day holding a sort of wake for Hattie, remembering good times, laughing and weeping. Kim and Joan stayed the night. We were all reluctant to part as if we were holding a piece of her with us before, inevitably, we had to let her go and deal with the cold reality of her loss. The next day we got on with all the preparations for her funeral. Kim wanted to get back to Eardley Crescent and resume his life there saying that if he didn't do it right away then he never would.

We went together. Martin was there and had started on some housework and I pitched in with him to make it as normal as we possibly could. Bruce came over and lots of other friends gathered but as crowded as the house was, it seemed like a shell. Bruce checked the fridge, which was bulging as usual. There were cold meats and vegetables from the last meal Hattie had prepared. He said that she would never forgive us if we didn't use up what was there and he made an enormous pan of soup for everybody and a plate of cold cuts and cheeses. It seemed important to keep busy, to use the house to comfort anyone who needed to come over, just as she would have done.

Hattie had died of a massive heart attack at the horribly young age of fifty-four. But with her weight to carry and the way she worked she did not make life easy for herself. She smoked incessantly; she used to say that she only lit up once a day and it was true: she just chain-smoked from then on, lighting one from the other throughout the day.

A few days later Robin arrived with his new bride whom we called Bun, as she had been a Bunny girl and any other way was too complicated. She was as pretty as a picture and all at sea in a strange world under such strange circumstances. I did my best to make her feel at home, like family, and she responded eagerly, although to tell the truth I felt, even after being with John for sixteen years, as if I too was on the periphery of things. I was also reluctant to appear pushy as if I was trying to take Hattie's place as the female head of the family. During that very grim week we all stayed close and busy, sorting out the funeral arrangements and so forth, and Bruce arranged to do the catering after the service.

Hattie was cremated at Chiswick. It was a simple ceremony, with no words intoned over her coffin, only music played softly on the piano in the chapel by her friend of many years, Peter Greenwell. He played all her favourite songs which seemed to bring her closer to us than ever. She had issued specific instructions in advance: no flowers, money to her favourite charities and a good piss-up afterwards, no tears. She might as well have asked the Thames to stop flowing. As we arrived at the cemetery there was a bunch of elderly ladies standing just outside the chapel. One of them touched John's arm as we passed and said, 'We know who you are, we all loved Hattie and we wanted to come and see her off.' John, deeply moved, said how kind of them and if there was room they were welcome to come and stand at the back. But they insisted that it was private and we went inside without them.

As we passed them on the way to our cars John once again thanked them for coming and one of them piped up with 'I don't suppose you could give us a lift to Fulham could you?' As there were about a dozen of them and all the spaces in the cars were full John had to say no, and as we got into the car John said, 'Hattie would have managed it somehow.'

One month later there was a memorial service for her at St Paul's in Covent Garden, known as the actor's church. It was a lovely occasion, packed with many famous people who loved her. John gave a tender and gently funny speech about her life. The regulars from the Players' sang together all the songs that had become her own over the years and Kenneth Williams gave a touching address ending with something from a book that Hattie had searched out for him the previous Christmas, knowing and remembering that he had once mentioned to her that it was out of print. It was a novel called *A Life for a Life* by Diana Maria Mulock (1826-87) and he quoted this passage from it, which sums her up perfectly:

Oh, the comfort, the inexpressible comfort of feeling safe with a person; having neither to weigh thoughts, nor measure words, but pour them all out just as they are, chaff and grain together, knowing that a faithful hand will take and sift them, keep what is worth keeping, and then, with a breath of kindness, blow the rest away.

The Christmas following Hattie's death I determined to make a celebration as lavish and as sumptuous as she had always done, in her honour. Robin was working so he and Bun could not be there but Jake came (somehow we had begun to call him that as his friends did) and David and Susie and Emma and my parents all gathered. I decorated the Ramsgate house with lights and a tree, bought lovely gifts for everyone, far too expensive and over the top but it had to be special to attempt to make a good memory to help diffuse the sadness of Hattie's loss. We tried our best and it was a good one.

Jake found presents that had been secreted away by Hattie earlier in the year already labelled, her thoughtfulness still reaching out to us. We had a big party on Boxing night where Jake was pulled by two raunchy local girls and was missing for most of the following day. We kept him with us as long as we could but he was eager to return to his lair at Eardley Crescent, theoretically empty now except for him. The old friend who had lived on the top floor, an actor called John Bailey who had been there for the past fifteen years, had also gone. He found it too sad without Hattie's presence, in any case the hangers-on around Jake had multiplied and were in danger of taking over the entire house.

Martin, who to everyone's amazement had been made executor of Hattie's will was, according to Jake, a ubiquitous and un-wanted presence about the place and things were not going too well. In the early months of 1981 we rented the basement flat at Eardley Crescent. Jake moved into the ground floor and John and I used the flat whenever we needed to be in town. I loved it. There were just two huge rooms, the living-room and the bedroom, both spacious and elegant. There was a kitchen and a bathroom along the hall where hung photographs of the family and lots of glamour photos of John and Hattie taken during the early days of their marriage.

According to Martin the house had to be sold as there were death duties and taxes to be paid. The boys inherited equally and as well as Eardley Crescent there was a house in Fulham, which had belonged to Hattie's mother who had died in the previous year. Her affairs were still unsettled and it was all a bit of a muddle but John and I felt that it was none of our business. The seaside house in Cliftonville had been sold some time earlier. It broke my heart to think of the London house being sold but it was too big for Jake and Robin was in LA. All those memories – Hattie had lived there most of her life and it seemed so sad – but life goes on. Eventually Jake moved into the smaller Fulham house and Eardley Crescent passed into the hands of somebody who sliced all the grand and airy rooms into little plywood units and crammed it full. I know this because a few years ago Comic Heritage, a charity who put blue plaques on houses where comedians and actors have lived, put a plaque on Eardley Crescent and some of us were allowed inside for interviews. The lovely living-room where so many wonderful Christmas parties had taken place was now half its size, the beautiful marble fireplace was gone and the soul of the house had fled. Even the hall was now narrowed to two grim tunnels, one leading upstairs and one down to the basement flat.

Once or twice if John had to work in town we stayed at the Fulham house but it was distressing to see a lovely house so neglected. It was dirty and untidy, none of Jake's 'friends' seemed to understand the rudiments of washing up or getting up, come to that. There were always people sleeping there, including Jake who never seemed to surface until the afternoon. I spent the time during my visits cleaning but it was hardly noticed and soon back to its normal chaos. I knew it was none of our business but our visits became less frequent and we decided to rent a flat in Notting Hill for a year instead although we never really got that much use out of it. Ramsgate had become the place we most wanted to be.

8

The Christmas of 1981 could hardly have
been more different from the year before.
We spent it with Robin who was touring
California with Rod Stewart. There were
two big concert venues over the holiday in
LA and San Francisco and Robin wanted us
to be present at both. As we had never seen
him onstage this seemed too good a chance
to miss. Bun was waiting for us as we
arrived at Los Angeles airport. Robin was
touring but had arranged for the three of us
to catch the Talgo train for San Francisco in
a couple of days in order to see the show.
That train journey was his treat. It was first
class, took ten hours and was unlike any
train ride we had ever taken before. There
was a luxury restaurant, a snack bar, a piano
bar and an observation lounge in the roof of
the train with revolving armchairs and
waiter service for drinks. Even the ladies rest
room was luxurious, with a private sitting-
room. It was curtain-up to a most lavish
interlude and our first real glimpse into the

life of the pop music world.

When we arrived at San Francisco Robin met us. We were booked into a grand hotel at the top of Nob Hill and the following night John and I saw our first pop concert. Before the show we were taken backstage to the hospitality room where there was booze and food in abundance and a party atmosphere prevailed. It was so different from the mood of an actor's dressing-room before a performance, where, in John's case at least, peace and tranquillity and solitude were essential. John couldn't even bear to be spoken to while waiting in the wings to make his entrance, while here the impression was that the more hyped up the boys were the better, like gladiators.

John and Bunny and I were taken just before the off to our seats at the side of the stage which was roped off strictly for VIPs. We were given stick-on labels and instructed not to let anyone take them off us as it would give them back-stage access. We were also told that we had to get out just before the end. The security was like a war summit meeting; bodyguards the size of tanks watched everything with eyes like eagles. The show was great: Robin was cool and relaxed, Rod leapt about like a teenager and the crowd was happily hysterical. So crazy, in fact, that half-way through the second set the barrier that was holding the crowd back from approaching too near the stage broke and the audience surged forward leaving us stuck at the side, marooned in the VIP box. There was no way that we could get through the sea of screaming fans so we were resigned to staying put and finding our own way back to the hotel. We were deafened by the decibels and almost scared. Suddenly, looming above the heads of the oblivious fans who were spellbound by the happenings on stage, a team of bodyguards appeared. To our great relief and humiliation we were lifted aloft and passed over the heads of the crowd to the back of the stage where a fleet of limousines was waiting, chauffeurs in place.

John was trembling and I was pretty stunned, added to which our hearing had gone. Bunny, a veteran of these affairs, was saying something apparently unmoved and in complete possession of her faculties, but we only saw her lips moving, the roar of the music still dominating our senses. The next moment the musicians appeared straight offstage. Clutching towels and pouring sweat they leapt into the waiting cars and we were off seconds after the last note had sounded – back to the sanctuary of the hotel. On the way the driver was playing pop music on the radio but Robin asked him to switch it off. He could not bear to hear any music at home during these tours, just occasionally something classical and serene, and we were not at all surprised.

At the hotel while Robin and the boys were showering and chilling out John and I went to the bar, still slightly deafened but impressed by the experience. It was not exactly our sort of music but great rock and roll – and exhilarating. John was proud of Robin and what he had achieved entirely through his own efforts. Later, after a light supper in the restaurant, Robin and most of the other musicians were taken to a suite at the top of the hotel to meet some minor princess who was a fan of Rod Stewart and a sort of groupie. She was married to a far eastern oil-rich prince who kept the suite permanently for his own use and employed six bodyguards, rumoured to be ex-SAS, for her personal protection. We were taken by private lift, accompanied by bodyguards with walkie-talkies who were stationed outside the door and at other strategic points around the hotel. I was told later that the prince had a hundred bodyguards of his own.

The suite had a dining-room which could seat twenty-eight people, a library which went up into the circular dome of the roof and a kitchen that could accommodate ten chefs. We were wined and waited on, there was a buffet of the richest fare from caviar upwards and a display of wealth that made me think of Ethiopia and of vulgarity. Needless to say we all became slightly tipsy and very friendly. Despite the surroundings it was a lovely opportunity to get to know the other musicians and technicians, who were a great bunch of lads. We ended the night with a sing song around the very grand piano with John playing Noël Coward standards like 'London Pride' and 'A Room With A View' until we were told politely by one of her staff that the princess had retired, and in other words would we all piss off.

We loved San Francisco. The following day Robin, John, Bun and I saw the sights, lunching at Fisherman's Wharf from where we could see Alcatraz prison across the bay. That night both of us took it very easy, the jet lag and the excitement of the concert having knocked us for six. John, in spite of being careful of his alcohol intake, admitted to having downed a few vodkas the previous night, so it was dinner in our room and early to bed for us while Robin, Bun and the boys did the whole thing all over again. In the morning the band flew back to LA together, getting to the airport by the customary limousines. We were followed by a car full of dedicated and noisy fans – apparently each band member had his own groupies.

Back in LA the tour continued. Sometimes Robin worked near enough to home to get back at night and sometimes not. John and I were cosy enough in their pretty house in Hollywood with all the modern comforts and the TV with all those stations and mad ads. There was also a pool which nobody would have dreamed of entering in December except John, one afternoon when he was at a loose end. We were told by a friend that the lovely English actor Freddie Jones was in town to make a film with Clint Eastwood. He appeared in films like *The Elephant Man* and *Far From the Madding Crowd*, and his distinguished TV appearances are too numerous to list. Like John he had a unique style. The film he was there for was *Firefox* and he was staying at the Holiday Inn. So we made contact and arranged to meet him there one afternoon. He was sitting alone in the dark empty bar with his back to the entrance when we arrived and looked the picture of dejection.

'Is that darling Freddie?' boomed John, and without looking round Freddie shouted back, 'Come over here and have something expensive with an umbrella in it quickly.'

We had a wonderful afternoon, three exiles lost in a strange land, making each other homesick, swapping yarns, swinging the lamp as they say. Freddie bemoaned the fact that throughout his career his dream had been to play Lear and in the very week that the part was finally offered, together with the chance of a season at the National Theatre for twopence-halfpenny a week, he had also been offered a TV comedy series *and* the Clint Eastwood film. Only one was possible; he hadn't worked for months and there are so few parts for fine actors, even of his calibre. After a week of breast-beating and weeping, he had to go for the money. He has a wife and two sons and actors have to eat. It's a funny old world when one looks at some of the frothy rubbish that's made for American TV and the fees that are earned by talentless Barbie dolls and action men. Here was dear Freddie about to earn a tidy sum to save the family fortunes and all but weeping at the lost and maybe last chance of playing Lear for peanuts. It gives one pause, as they say. But that's a proper actor for you. Occasionally Freddie would rise to his feet and give a rendering of Browning's 'Oh to be in England now that April's there', or quote from Rupert Brooke, 'God, I must rise and catch a train, and get me to England once again'. I'm sure no one working there was aware that two fine actors and Englishmen had graced that dreary bar with their presence that afternoon.

The last show of the tour was in LA and this time we were taken from our Beverley Hills hotel to the venue by an English double-decker bus. On the way drinks were served and songs were sung and backstage the lavish entertainment continued. When it was time for the boys to go on they were escorted on to the stage by a massed band of Scottish pipers in full-kilted regalia, an incredible sight. This time Bunny, John and I watched from the gallery at the back of the stadium, in a section from which we could make our own way backstage at the end of the show. When Tina Turner did a couple of numbers with Rod the crowd went wild. It was a great show and we were so carried away that we three little Cinderellas did not leave the ball early enough and we missed the bus which couldn't wait for time or tide. By the time we arrived backstage there was pandemonium, no taxis, roadies packing up and outside thousands of yelling and swarming fans.

We peeled off our pass IDs and got swept along with the crowd until we came to a hotel where, after an eternity we managed to get a taxi home. That's show business, one day up there with the greats, the next trailing in the gutter, or at any rate standing in line for a cab like anyone else. A few nights before Christmas Rod Stewart gave a party to mark the end of the tour. It was a lavish affair held at his rather swanky house. The drive was lined with flunkies in knee breeches holding flaming torches to greet us on arrival. In the entrance hall, as our coats were taken, we were given ice-cold slugs of Russian vodka and caviar.

The house was enormous, and the whole place twinkled with stars. To my great delight I spotted Gregory Peck, who Robin said was Rod's neighbour and a totally good fellow, and Farah Fawcett with Ryan O'Neal. There was a pre-Raphaelite room, a Tiffany room and a ballroom in the centre of which was a Christmas tree, which reached to the roof. At the far end was a minstrels' gallery housing a jazz group to which John gravitated immediately and where he spent a great deal of the evening sitting among the jazzmen.

It was a magical night, kept steady, sane and real by Rod's family who had come over to spend Christmas with him. His mum, a great old lady in a wheelchair, said to John, 'Our boys have done us proud, John.' There were aunts and uncles all having a great time and among all those stars they brought a breath of home and reality.

During that holiday John and Robin grew closer than before. Bun and I left them alone at times and went shopping together as there were things that were private between them which needed to come to the surface. John's guilt at not being there much during his sons' childhood was just one of them. He needed to get things off his chest and talk about Hattie and express and share that sense of loss that no one else could know. Bun and I grew close as well: she became a sort of surrogate daughter and still is even though the marriage to Robin ended after fifteen years. But not the friendship. We Le Mesuriers stick together. Now Robin and Robin are like brother and sister and I remind them that I am now the oldest member of the family and my will must be obeyed.

Back in England a period of quiet set in, as is usual in the grey month of January. John and Derek continued to make contact and John did the odd job for radio, which kept him in touch with the business, but it was a fallow period financially. The trip to America had all but cleaned us out despite the fact that we were Robin's guests. There had been travelling expenses, we'd wanted to be generous with our thank yous, and of course in feckless holiday mode we bought a few little things for ourselves. It had been a wonderfully restorative time as in the previous year a lot of friends had died. Peter Sellers, the director Seth Holt and Bill Evans, the brilliant American pianist to whom John was so devoted. Whenever he was in town playing at Ronnie Scott's I used to call myself a Bill Evans widow. So we felt the pinch for a while back in Blighty, but we never regretted the LA trip, especially as the rest of that year had left us with few happy memories, as is reflected in this exchange of letters between Derek and John.

My Dear John,

I have meant to write so many times for so many reasons. Such an unhappy year in so many ways but for now, while we live, let our thoughts be for the living.

I am in London twice a week now and due to recent events in New York I have had *to change* home number to ********* (a trusting friend passed my old one to the *News of the World* as a favour!)

It would be nice to have lunch soon.

Thanks for the card 'Old friend'.

Love to all.

'Old' Derek

8 London Road
Ramsgate

Dear Derek,

I was so pleased to get your letter. Also the change of telephone numbers as from Sudbury and indeed the Chelsea Number. I have noted them and will not forget them.

You see, we are *still* surrounded by knowing prats who divulge your privacy and at the same time believe they are being of some kind of service to you. I recall the Lennon episode, in your case for instance when the *News of the World* went to work on you.

Last Saturday morning at 3 am, the bell rang and there was someone breathing heavily through the letterbox, saying that he had met me in Tregunter Road, Earls Court, in 1950, and had something he wanted to show me.

We called the police and he was sent merrily on his way. But nobody needs this, and it is also a bit alarming when the bell rings at such an hour, you are asleep and your wife has to cope with it.

I am so glad last year is over and done with, so many of my loved ones disappeared, and it was a sod from a professional point of view.

I am doing *The Lord of the Rings* on Radio. This I do not understand too well. It is a bit too fey for me, but I have friends like Michael Hordern, Ian Holm, and Robert Stephens in it as well. *They* don't quite understand it either! I'll remember about lunch in the New Year.

In the meantime, love,

John

Early in 1982 there were plans for John and Arthur Lowe to do a radio series written by Michael Knowles and Harold Snoad, who had directed *Dad's Army*. Called *It Sticks Out Half a Mile*, it was to be a spin-off of the TV series set in the post-war era, in which Arthur and John as Mainwaring and Wilson had bought a dilapidated pier and gone into business together. John and Arthur did a pilot episode which was well received by the BBC powers that be and plans went ahead to do a series of ten episodes, with Ian Lavender and Bill Pertwee in the cast as well. John was excited at the thought of working with Arthur again but it was obvious that he wasn't in robust health at the time. The trip to America had tired him; he succumbed to a bad case of influenza and needed careful nursing and a sensible diet free of alcohol and fried food to get him back on his feet. He wrote to Arthur at this time:

How very nice to hear from you,

I feel very lonely without you all sometimes and am sad not to be busy as you are, but the slightest physical exertion puffs me out and I've accepted that my defection was inevitable.

Mind you, if we were all called on location to Thetford tomorrow, I'd be there.

John

John's friendship with Arthur may not have been quite as close as the ones he had with Jimmy Beck and Clive Dunn, but looking forward to working with him really cheered John up. There was also talk of turning the new show into a TV series if the ratings were good. The scripts certainly were, so with something promising for the future John was able to recover and enjoy the spring in Ramsgate with a light hopeful heart.

That Easter was a happy one. The whole family came to stay, my granddaughter was by then two years old and loved Ramsgate and our big garden. She called me Ganga, a name which has stuck to me ever since; so John and I were now Ganga and Bod while Kim was Jake, and we all grew into our new names easily. I hired a movie camera to record the celebrations and I'm glad I did as we still have those lasting memories of a happy time around the table in the garden, and of John in his red leather armchair reading to his 'friend and wife' 'The Love Story of Alfred J. Prufrock' by T.S. Eliot, one of my favourite poems. Not that he did it willingly as poetry wasn't his thing at all, but he did it to please me. He read it blind, so to speak, and at first you can see in the little home movie that he could not make much sense of it. But half-way through he got the meaning of it. Perhaps he saw something of himself in Alf Prufrock because at the end of the poem when he came to 'Till human voices wake us, and we drown', he looked into the camera and there were tears in his eyes.

Once, when we were first married and just after Eliot's death, a benefit and tribute was staged for his widow Vivien. John was asked to read something from 'Sweeney Agonistes', an unpublished speech that for some reason had been omitted from the original text. He turned it down flat until he found that Cleo Laine and John Dankworth had set it to jazz and that he would be required to do it in recitative, or talking to music in a Rex Harrison way. Now he leapt at it with the speed of a greyhound leaving the trap. He was among august company; Peter O'Toole read Prufrock, Groucho Marx read 'Gus The Theatre Cat' and the list of other celebrity contributors was long and strong. I had heavy cold so I missed it and regret it to this day. I regret even more the fact that at a party, John lent the LP resulting from that evening, one of a very limited number edition, to a woman choreographer and it hasn't been seen from that day to this, in spite of several pleas from John for its return. John was constantly foisting music and books on to people and it always made me cross when things were not returned.

That Easter, however, was recorded on film and I have never been tempted to lend that particular item out to anybody. People still ask me if I get upset at watching John on TV repeats and I reply truthfully that I don't at all. It's lovely to see him on that screen alive and doing what made him happy, but the home movies are different because they are so private and personal.

Easter 1982 was also John's 70th birthday. It seemed, on paper, that he had reached a considerable age but he did not look any different to me. John was one of those men – it is usually men, in my observation – whose face and features were somehow formed and set in childhood and as a result he didn't look particularly youthful as a young man or change much as he grew older.

Sudbury,
Suffolk.
April 7 1982

Dear John,

Sorry I missed your birthday. Well done. It must be idiotic for you to face such a relative truth. I am sure you remember your first day of school and all those recent landmarks. It's well known that the past is getting ever closer. Barbara Wootton said on TV that life to her seemed astonishingly short. She is eighty-five. I am fifty next month. Outrageous! Errol Flynn was fifty when he passed over into another place. He did *seem* older. He used to put cocaine on his penis, so your old friend David Niven says. That would make a much more interesting ad for Maxwell House or Nescafe or whatever it is don't you think?

This Dardanelles [I think he must have been referring to the Falklands] business is a bit thick don't you think? I think Mrs Thatcher's Head Must Roll. Unless Reagan can get her out of the mess it *will* and I would give it an extra kick down the hill just for the education cuts alone...

Yes, what a *great* idea for you to publish your letters [this was something John had suggested to Derek]. Go to it now. Have mine if you want, most honoured... Mumble, mumble, all of that.

Just let me have a last look for libel or embarrassing abuse if you *do* go ahead. Those slim volumes, properly illustrated, edited, bound, published and well marketed can be terrific fun.

Do you like *Hi De Hi*? I don't know why, but I would very much like to have your opinion on this burning issue? Answer soon please. I saw you in one of those soundtracks with a series of expensive sets attached the other night ... Worthing, or some such thing. You were as loveable as ever despite your script, and it was good to see you. God: If only I could write ... I would make a fortune.

That's it for now John. I am preparing for 3.32pm. 'And now we go over live to Westminster *where* the Foreign Secretary is putting cocaine on his penis ... I'm sorry I'll read that again ... where the House is debating the Falkland Isles.'

Oh, yes ... would it be OK (this is a genuine afterthought). Would it be OK if I were to use a couple of your letters in a book I'm writing? You could see them of course it goes without saying) in case there's something rude about Bryan Forbes or Duncan (not Harry) Weldon.

Love as ever to one and all.

Derek & Joan

8 London Road
Ramsgate
April 11th

My Dear Derek,

It was lovely to get your funny and witty letter on the morning of Maundy Thursday.

Chaos was reigning in my home when I started to read it.

The situation was not unlike Dunkirk on a small scale, people coming and going, and trying in the manner of 'Melpomenus Jones' to get the hell out of it!

Voices were raised, the local railway station alerted.

All this coupled with an enchanting female child of two years who, in the midst of the consternation appeared to be bent on 'throwing a shit fit', needless to say, she succeeded admirably.

Anyway, Joan and I in particular are heaving some sighs of relief after this minuscule holocaust.

The relief was not to last. A phone call from Herne Bay, tells us that Susie (mother of the beautiful child) has left her London flat key behind, could someone get the keys for her to pick them up some 4 stations beyond Herne Bay!

David, my stepson, and the father of the child took off in a taxi and the mission was successfully completed, and he has just returned having hitched a lift in a hearse.

It is interesting you should ask me what I think of *Hi De Hi*, there is obviously something wrong with it, cannot put my finger on it but I think the answer *could* be that it is too real. When you view it, you are overcome with horror, in what goes on in those places. A little peep into hell perhaps?

I am doing in the near future a guest appearance on this particular program, so perhaps I shall be able to give you a more considered view on the whole proceedings.

I do think it is the best thing Croft and Petty have turned out since *Dad's Army*.

Mrs Lowsborough–Goodby, poor old thing, has recently been given another airing by Terry Wogan, Jimmy Young and Benny Green, so there must be a little interest left about the Album we tried to do together all those years ago*; and I will, if I may pick up a few of them as and when it is possible.

Your letters keep me sane. Alun Owen sends love. I did one of his Radio plays in Cardiff recently.

As always,

John

This was written at the end of that lovely Easter week we had all spent together at Ramsgate. The shit fit was thrown by my granddaughter Emma, who did not want to

* *What is Going to Become of Us All?*

leave Bod and Ganga's house and go back to London, and who could blame her? You can imagine why that clumsy home movie is so precious to me: the family was lovingly gathered, we had much to celebrate and perhaps we all seemed to experience the intensity of pleasure in it all because just over the horizon things were about to change…

In the summer of 1982 Arthur Lowe died suddenly in his dressing room. It was between the matinée and the evening performance of R.C. Sherriff's *Home from the Sea*. He was reading a book when he collapsed. John was very saddened: it seemed that everyone John had loved and been close to was going too early. Arthur was only sixty-six. The only consolation was that he went out in harness. Any actor worth his salt, said John, would want to go suddenly still working at the thing he loved. One remembers Tommy Cooper and Leonard Rossiter who both went that way and can only hope that they are happily observing things from 'the gods'. John spoke at Arthur's memorial service, airing a tribute to his old friend and commanding officer. Now the company was truly disbanded: *Dad's Army* was no more.

However, *It Sticks out Half a Mile* continued with Bill Pertwee taking Arthur's place and ten more episodes were recorded. In the autumn of that sad year John was asked to write his memoirs. There was little work to distract him as it was a lean period so it was a good time to do something different. He would work at his desk in his bedroom and in the evening would read out what the day had produced. It was just the same routine as when he was learning his lines and it kept him occupied and quite cheerful.

By then we had given up most of our ties with London. Ramsgate was now our only home and we were settled into it quite happily. Occasionally we would have the odd shopping trip to London for John's clothes and haircuts. Simpsons, Turnbull & Asser for shirts and other items, Jackie at Ramon in Kensington for the hair – he was rightly proud, almost vain – about that abundant white hair of his. John was a joy to shop with, no waffling at all. He had an unerring knack of going straight to the best quality garment. Out of a row of jackets he would pick a cashmere check which cost a fortune but was just perfect. Turnbull & Asser had just the right shirts, long sleeves, broad shoulders, good cotton and the strongest colours. Red was his favourite, there was always something red about his person, be it socks, silk handkerchief or a lining. Scarves were another love of his, cashmere or silk only, and once again in the strong colours which suited him. He would pick out what he wanted then head for a pub in Jermyn Street leaving me to deal with the bill.

One Christmas I bought him six enormous silk handkerchiefs from Turnbull & Asser in wonderful colours. He loved a handkerchief tumbling out of his breast pocket. Very common, he said, to sport a folded handkerchief. A few days after Christmas I found the handkerchiefs in the dustbin covered with frost, consigned there innocently due to his knack of clearing away wrapping paper as soon as the gift was revealed. The Christmas of 1983 was to be his last and happily most of the family were together again. Robin was touring but Jake came and we had many funny times. On Christmas Day, David, Jake and John got drunk and high and had a jam session with John on the piano. It sounded great, but then, I was high and drunk too.

That New Year the correspondence with

Derek was still in full flow:

Sudbury,
Suffolk
March 12, 1983

My Dear John

Thank you very much for the books; *nobody* returns books, yet *you* did! I have done about 120,000 words of a new one, much calmer and more literate and not so alarming. Funnier in places, I think but certainly much more serious. I note your comments about your 'comedy' series and have pleasure, an acrid pleasure but pleasure nonetheless, in enclosing a little piece by the great Barry Took on comedy. It really is too bad. *Is* it what the public wants? I'm not convinced it is but it is certainly what they get. It is this awful business of the laugh-punctuated bang-bang-bang script; you can turn your back to the set and it doesn't matter what's happening, the laughter ripples through, hyena-like. I hate it very much. I sometimes think it's Jealousy – seems such an easy way for the writers to make money but it isn't Jealousy and it isn't easy. It is that it isn't funny. I wanted to write a series called: Was Hitler a Pansy? But I couldn't get any further than the title for laughing. So who am I to talk? Thank you for your message from Maurice Cole (alias Kenny Everett) of Crosby. I am glad to have his number; we used to be good friends but now he has taken to female and other impersonation, I'm not sure I know him. Barry T. is rather hard on him but I think there may be some truth in it. Once glance from Max Wall is worth the whole of any series. Have you read *his* book? I have. Simple and charming. He has had some life; I'm bound to say. (*Bound* to say.

Why *bound* to say? It reminds me of something you once said you had said when someone else said:

'The show *must* go on!' You simply said 'why?') *Very* good.

'Why' Funnier than fifty episodes of 'I Ain't Half a Card!' or some such. By the way I remember having a terrible time extricating myself from a dispute with a woman from *Woman's Own* who said to me: 'I must talk to you. I need to talk to Mary Hopkins for ten minutes.' I must have had a trying day because I went absolutely white, even pale green or death blue with intense rage and hissed at her: '*Need*, you need to talk to Mary

Hopkins. How can anyone *NEED* to talk to Mary Hopkins? It may be desirable, advantageous or even helpful but you can't possibly *need* to talk to Mary Hopkins. Why do you abuse the language *and* waste my time?' She wasn't a bad woman at all, certainly experienced and courteous. I tried to pull out of the anger but it took quite some time and I had quite lost the confidence of the poor woman by the time I *had* calmed down. (I had had some LSD at the time, he adds with languor. My sidekick told me I had 'over-reacted'. They were mad days – 1968.)

Where is Shergar? Not round here. There isn't a single hedge high enough to hide a pit pony round here any more. Those terrible hedging machines have done their absolute worst this year. I am going to complain to the National Front about it. They know how to take care of things like that. 'Skinheads for the Countryside.'

I must close now. I am late for tea, I think. It is already dark and dogs are howling over the meadows.

Lots of love to one and all who are in on the Joke.

Derek

P.S. Keep writing your book EVERY DAY

even 100 words! Even 10 words. Even *one*.

In the spring John got a script for a TV play starring Anthony Hopkins, with whom he shared a profound friendship. It was called *A Married Man* by Piers Paul Read and there was a lovely part for John as Hopkins's father-in-law. They had strong, long scenes together in which they talked of their beliefs and convictions. One was as they were walking through a garden and perfect timing was imperative, so John and I spent hours walking around *our* garden, pacing his steps and rehearsing his lines. He spent a week on location in Bristol and I went with him. We arrived on a Saturday to settle in for Monday and saw that Tom Baker was doing *Educating Rita* at the local theatre. It was the last performance and we rang the desk using John's name and begged to be squeezed in although the house was sold out. We were fortunate to catch him as it was a lovely performance. He and John were old Soho mates and we both loved him. We had dinner afterwards; it was to be the last time they saw each other. Strange how sometimes every detail that presages a momentous event is preserved in perfect memory, even though one could not have known what was to come.

Also in 1983 I went on a week's holiday to Spain with David, Susie and Emma. A cousin moved into the Ramsgate house to look after John and the cats, none of whom had mastered the knack of opening a can of food. During my absence Robin was passing through London, doing a gig at Earls Court, and John went up with my cousin to see the show and spend some time afterwards with his son. I believe that he may have had a few more drinks than usual as he stayed quite late into the small hours and hired a car to take them back to Ramsgate. According to my cousin he cried on the way home and was tired and melancholy the following day. I arrived back from Spain that evening and although having planned to spend the night in London at David and Susie's I changed my mind on arrival. The others opted to come with me by taxi to spend the night in Ramsgate and go back to London by train as they both wanted to see John too. Something instinctive was happening.

In Ramsgate the house was in darkness. Both John and my cousin had gone to bed early after being out so late on the previous night. When we arrived we woke them, of course, and in spite of the disturbance John was pleased to see me. He hugged me tight and said, 'I've felt very ill this past week but now you're here I shall be better.'

The following day everyone left, much to John's relief, as he wanted to be peaceful. I made him a good dinner that night and although he seemed tired he was happy enough. Early next morning he began to haemorrhage. He was rushed to Ramsgate hospital, mercifully a stone's throw away, where he was made comfortable. The six years of forbidden good living had caught up with him. From then on it was a salt-free diet and no more alcohol. The following four months were spent in and out of hospital as his liver was terminally damaged. I didn't want to believe that there was no hope and thought that diet would once again do the magic trick and pull him round. The continuing letters to and from Derek certainly gave him pleasure and little patches of last strength.

Sudbury
Just a little later. September

My Dear John,

I was going to visit you with some hard-boiled eggs and nuts last week after returning from the wonders of mid and North Wales but left it too late as it turns out since your most welcome letter received today shows you to be out and home. Well done squire!

I am just delighted and (seemingly turning pink in the ribbon.) I hope and pray on the life of Morrie Geyer (see enclosed) that you will make sufficient progress to be able to attend the getting to know you party for Sir Fred Pontin which the Bryan Forbeses are giving at the Goodtime Café over Larry's The Hairdresser's in Virginia Water. The Five Fallopians are performing their incredible 'tube' dance and we are hoping to get old Billy Nevitt along to represent 'The North' and give us some tips for the November handicap.

I am still amazed to realise that Lester isn't the Boy Wonder any more.

Thirty-five years in the saddle and still bumping. But never boring. I loved a Jeff Barnard story about Piggot. They were driving through Newmarket when … (or was it Lambourn? Anyway…) they were driving and they saw a loose horse in the road, alone. 'We should get hold of that,' said Jeff. 'Never,' said Lester. 'Get hold of a loose horse and you end up holding the facking thing all facking day.'

Asked by Kosset carpets whether he would like the gift of one of their celebrated white cats, for work on a commercial, Piggot is said to have replied: 'A cat? I'd rather have a facking monkey.' I backed him in every race one season in the late sixties and lost quite a lot of money on the year.

I enclose, as I have noted, a thing my old friend Geo H sent me from Beverley Hills. It's the only copy I have so when you have noted the address and ordered your shirt(s) would you be a good chap and let me have it back.★ I will Xerox it then and let you have your own copy. I have, for your inform- ation, ordered the ecru, the soft brown and the dusty rose, so if you want to choose outside that range, it might be best in case we should meet and 'clash' one day, who knows, at a Happy Hundredth party for Lew Grade.

Thank you John for warm and flattering asides in your book. You may of course use that letter if you wish, if you think it funny

★ S.a.e. Enclosed, Hard times dictate that jokes are only *on lone* now. Felt I had to rush this one to you

enough. Would suggest you be more economical with the underlinings (indicating Italics) than I was.

Derek

My dear Derek

Thank you so much for your letter.
Your letters never let me down.
As for the enclosure which I return (guard it with your life) it made me laugh to such an extent that I spilled some rice crispies and milk all over the kitchen table.
Apart from the wording of the ad itself, looking closely at the face reminded me somewhat of Bill Pertwee with touch of Ernie Wise thrown in for good measure.
Take another look and see what you think.

Love to all.

John

That September John was taken into King's College Hospital in south London for more treatment. To be near him I stayed with Mark, my ex-husband, and his wife, Diana, who were two towers of strength during that time. Diana would run me to the hospital every day and pick me up later. She let me use her kitchen to cook John elaborate meals of anything he fancied, which was OK with the hospital as they could see that he didn't fancy their food much. He may have known somehow that he was beginning to die but did not want to acknowledge this, let alone discuss it, and I respected that wish. In many ways this was typical of so many occasions in his life when he had gone into 'hedgehog mode', as he termed it, and just curled up for self-protection. He did not really want much contact with other people – but there were some special friends who knew how bad things were.

Sudbury

My Dear John,

Just a few lines to say I am very distressed to hear all this and want you to know that I will be dropping in with half a dozen friends this week for a 'getting to know you' party at the bedside. Bryan Forbes suggested it and I have gathered some really fabulous people including Thea Alba from overleaf, her husband Diamante the armless pianist and Rovera the dog woman who was brought up by corgis in Norfolk before going into the business.

We thought we'd bring some music and have some fun. Tell the nurses we are a jolly lot who know how to have a good time and no messing!

I am very busy finishing a book on public sector borrowing requirement? Are you 'into' this kind of stuff? It is to do with over-shoot and under spend and a lot of other rather fascinating stuff. It makes a change from who's shagging who in Copulation Street.

In some seriousness I am supposed to be through with my very windy life story this week. I have five years yet to write having just had your party at the Savoy and met Frank Sinatra at Cubby Broccoli's house in Stepney, or was it Belgravia?

I would like to write 'the end' on the entire story and pick up a million pounds from the nearest cash point and bugger off but life was never said to be a bed of roses, as Kathleen (Huggins) Harrison said to Jack Warner.

It interested me to note that both you and Bella Lugosi have appeared with Elderly

Matron Riley.

I tried to talk to Kitty once but she was 'out'.

That's it my dear friend. I hope you improve steadily.

I shall return.

Derek

Derek wrote this to John when he was in hospital. A little later John replied:

8 London Road
Ramsgate
September 7, 1983

My Dear Derek,

Your letters have been a joy to me. Thank you so much. When I was in Hospital I read aloud a few extracts to some well-chosen Nurses who fell about. I have been at home now for about two weeks, and feel a lot better and look a lot better so I am told. I sometimes walk to the local pub and have a Lemonade and Bitter Lemon. People are very kind and thoughtful and tell me that they are pleased to see me 'about again' and then proceed to give me a blow-by-blow account of their *own* ailments. All of which is not too riveting but 'well meant' as my Mother used to say. I tend to think twice before venturing far without Joan near at hand. She has been marvellously helpful and patient throughout all this carry on.

I bash on with the book as best I can and am trying to view the whole project objectively. It is not always easy, as you must know, to do this. Bad days and good days come and go, and I can only trust the good days outweigh the bad ones.

I go back to the Hospital on September 20th for a check up. Just 'one night only', I hope they will change my diet a little which at the moment has to be 'salt free' not always easy for Joan to cope with.

I wonder if I could ask you to get the Guildford people to send a few copies of our Album. It was played recently on one of the all-night shows and several of the Nurses in Hospital on duty at the time heard it and were rather cross when their alarm bell rang in the middle and they had to go and attend to some patient who required the use of a bed pan. I would, if possible, like to give them a couple when I next go in.

With love to you both,

John

Two months after the first, John had another haemorrhage and this time was rushed straight to King's in London. Mark and David were visiting when it happened and were a comfort and a support. Mark was able to drive David and me to the hospital behind the ambulance so that we could arrive at the same time.

John had slipped into a coma and knew nothing of the journey, which was a blessing. Like the hedgehog, which he likened himself to, he was again able to curl himself away from the reality of what was happening and shut himself away. At one point as I sat with him in the hospital, I held his hand and said in his ear, 'If you can hear me squeeze my hand,' which he did. I told him that he was in hospital in London, and would be fine, I was with him and not to worry. Suddenly he said, 'National Health?' 'Yes,' I said. 'Thank God,' said John quite clearly, and went into a peaceful sleep.

Once more I stayed with Mark and Diana who were unstintingly helpful and kind to me. I was driven to the hospital each morning and picked up each evening, which cannot have been easy for them, but they loved John unconditionally, which helped, and they were family to us. I wrote in my epilogue to John's book, *A Jobbing Actor*, that our divorces never managed to sever the love we had for each other; our clan just grew branches. Sharing the pain of imminent bereavement made us close ranks even more tightly and Diana, though now divorced from Mark, is still one of my closest friends. Their children are part of the same tree and on it goes. Perhaps we have just been lucky or chosen our partners wisely with real love rather than the superficial kind, which is based on lust. I don't know, but I did count myself blessed and kept aloft during that awful time.

By now I realized that John was terminally ill. I had been told by the doctor not in so many words that the haemorrhage would happen again and could be fatal. Strangely I put the fact from my mind and dealt only with what had to be done each day and lived completely for and in the moment. His diet, his comfort and his needs occupied my time. To have dwelt on the future and my fears as to how his end would be and when it would come would have been impossible to endure. So somehow strength was given to me and consequently life became simple. I didn't ever wish to be anywhere else or think beyond the needs of the day. John was allowed home to Ramsgate and we had the odd guest to keep everything normal. Annie Ross, Peter Campbell, David, Susie and Emma. But mostly we were alone. John still worked on his book when he had the energy and, so far as he was concerned, it was a convalescence period, or so we both pretended to believe. Derek kept up his cheerful correspondence and John replied promptly.

The final haemorrhage happened in November. This time he was taken back to Ramsgate hospital. There was nothing more to be done. Outside the ward I gave way to despair and wept. An irritatingly cheerful nurse put her arm round me, saying 'This isn't like you, you are always so positive.' I did a lot of silent chanting in the following week and lived in the hospital, only going home to sleep. David and Jake came down and Mark and Diana came on the Sunday before he died to say goodbye. Mark was on the receiving end of John's last joke. As Mark bent over him he woke up. 'My dear fellow, you've grown a beard,' said John.

'Yes, I'm doing *Educating Rita* and I thought the beard might make me appear more intelligent,' replied Mark. 'And did it?' said John with a twinkle in his eye.

After they left he said, 'I'm fed up of it, darling. It's all been rather lovely, but I would like to go now.' I kissed his cheek and sat with him and he fell asleep quite quickly.

I could see that he had decided to die, and that all our pretence was over. I didn't have to be cheerful any more. The next morning he was in a coma, and he never woke from that sleep. I sat with him all day. At the end of the ward was a TV and that afternoon they showed *Where the Spies Are* which he had made in Nice with David Niven all those years before. On screen he was tanned and happy. We were courting at the time and he was in love, I think.

When I left that night to get some sleep, I asked the nurses to ring me immediately if anything happened. They rang at six in the morning. John's breathing had changed and it was fortunate that the hospital was only a hundred yards away so I was there in a flash. His breathing was harsh and he was near the end. I whispered a thank you for my lovely life into his ear. 'It's all waiting for you, darling,' I said. 'Let go now and be happy.' John's breathing stopped almost at once. I hoped that they were there, all his friends, Hattie, Peter Sellers, Arthur Lowe. I hoped it would be true. One morning during his illness he had dreamed that Arthur was standing by the bed, 'Come on, John,' he had said. 'We're all here waiting, but don't tell Joanie.' When he had opened the French windows the next morning a blackbird had hopped into the room. When John told me this I went cold and the Romany blood in me knew it had to be an omen. And here it was. Here was that rainy day. He was gone. All those light and gentle years of his company were over.

I walked back to my house on a fine morning and at the kitchen table I sat in his chair and wept for the past and my loss. Then I picked up the phone and gathered the tribe together.

Epilogue

Dear John,

I am sitting by a swimming pool. The sun is hot. I'm in Portugal, the Algarve, where we spent happy holidays with the Dunns. Seventeen years have passed since you ambled away from me on that sunny morning in November, yet you have seldom been far away.

So many things have happened that it's hard to know where to begin, so I'll go back to that day, 16 November 1983, and try to remember it all in sequence. Back to the saddest of all days when the news of your death began to circulate out like a ripple of gloom through family, friends and into the outside world.

It seemed that David, Jake, Susie and Emma were with me in no time. Emma gave me some flowers and said, 'This is so you won't be sad about Bod,' which made me cry all over again.

Diana pelted down the motorway the

moment she heard. Mum and Dad were in Spain but we got word out there as soon as we could. However, the news had already filtered through via a holidaymaker who had heard it on the radio.

The family had persuaded me to put in the *Times* obituary that you had 'conked out'. It was one of your often-repeated requests, 'Tell them I conked out, or snuffed it.' So all of us decided to honour it thus:

John Le Mesurier wishes it to be known that he conked out on November 16th. He sadly misses family and friends.

It was picked up by the rest of the media before the announcement was printed. Stuffily the *Times* refused it so it went into the *Telegraph* instead. By that evening it was on the billboards: 'Tell them I conked out,' said *Dad's Army* star. People were ringing from the press and the Beeb. Sue Pollard whom I hadn't met, rang from the bar of the BBC to say that there was a wake for John in progress and the general consensus of opinion was that the announcement had given people a smile to diffuse the sadness at losing you.

Peter Campbell had tried to talk me out of

it but the family stood firm: it was your wish, and it was honoured as you requested.

What a strange, unreal day it was. Diana, after making sure that I was all right and not about to shatter into pieces, tore off to London again and the rest of us stayed close. You were never absent for a minute and the evening was punctuated by tears and laughter alternately.

Jake and David were just great, reminiscing about you and keeping my spirits up. David remembered the time in the Savoy restaurant in Grange Road, Ramsgate, where you used the bar because it was a peaceful place to read your paper. One evening you and he were having a drink together as the diners began to arrive for their aperitifs and you both began to guess what each of the diners would drink. 'Sweet sherry and a large scotch,' you'd say as two more approached the bar, then you'd wait to hear their order. Most of the time you got it right as well. 'Here comes a gin and lime and a brown ale,' you'd say. Apparently you both got the giggles and as more people arrived you got sillier in your guessing what they would ask for.

Susie cooked dinner and made everything cosy, and friends kept calling. I drank too much, and Emma was angelic. Derek Taylor rang and we talked a long while. He said that he would like to come to his old friend's funeral, which got the family to planning. We wanted to get it just right, how you would have wanted it.

The next morning the papers were full of you. Marvellous things were said. The editorial in the *Guardian* was dedicated to you. The editor said that in the early films such as the Boultings and the Elstrees there was always one shining Le Mesurier moment that bound you to him with hoops of steel. How about that then! You were likened to a national treasure.

The number of letters of condolence was overwhelming. After your fashion I eventually answered every one and in *my* fashion I've kept most of them. Here are just a few...

Twickenham Film Studios
18th November 1983

Dear Mrs John

We were both greatly distressed to hear about John.

We had known him for so many years and

we are acutely conscious that words are entirely inadequate to express the sympathy we feel for you in your loss, and the genuine affection, respect and admiration we both had for him. In his quiet, gentle and invariably amusing way, he brought a warm glow and a marvellous sense of fun to the lives of others. He was not only a superbly professional artist; he was above all a splendid human being and an inspiration to all those who knew him. We share with you not merely grief, but a sense of joy which he generated in abundance.

Our warmest sympathy.

Sincerely,

John and Roy Boulting

P.S. please forgive us for being unable to attend the service on Monday. With a film being urgently lined up, we believe that John would understand, and accept our absence.

Tom Baker
Chateau Marmont,
Sunset Boulevard,
Hollywood.
L.A.
Wed, Nov 29th

Dear Joan,

Conked out!

Naturally I thought of the last time we met in Norwich and you and John were so kind about *Educating Rita.*

Conked out. How entirely John and how generous of you to repeat it.

I'll think of John and when you and I meet next we'll drink something – my memory is good at memories, of John and of you.

Today I go to Boston, on the 24th I'm in Chicago and from 29th I'm at the above address. If the boys are in LA I'll do champagne, tell them.

Love,

Tom B.

Frank Williams
17th November 1983

My dear Joan,

I was so very sorry to hear the news about John, he will be greatly missed by a large number of people.

I shall always feel it was a great privilege to have been in *Dad's Army* with him, and to have had the opportunity to experience his warmth, humour and on many occasions his great kindness. He really was a lovely man.

My friend Betty joins with me in sending our sympathy to you and to all John's family and we want to know we are all thinking of you.

Much love,

Frank (Williams)

And this from Alec Guinness, indicating that he too remembered those early days when they left their tap-dancing shoes behind and stepped forward on to wider stages.

November 1983

Dear Mrs Mesurier

I have recently returned from the continent and was greatly shocked to hear of John's death, please accept heart felt condolences.

I barely knew him, though we had a brief encounter in the film *Our Man in Havana* and I remember Carol Reed saying, 'I've *got* to get him for this part, he's my favourite comedian.' We were students together for a short time at the Fay Compton studio and I remember his very first work there, which seemed to all as brilliant and accomplished as his later and famous work. He was a delightful actor, with a lighter and wittier touch than anyone I can think of.

I do wish I had got to know him, he will be sadly missed by all in the profession.

I wish you courage and hope and peace of mind

Yours sincerely

Alec Guinness

During the week before your funeral the family stood round me like a ring of sturdy

312

trees. Jake and David planned your send-off and Susie helped me with your clothes and possessions. We recycled most things back into the family: your lovely scarves were shared between Mark, the navy polka dot which he wears to this day as his lucky mascot, and David, who chose the pastel coloured silk one that I bought for your birthday one year. Jake had the cashmere and silk reversible and Susie and I had the plain cashmere ones, yellow for Susie to match her fair hair, and the red for me to wear your favourite colour.

Gradually your things became our talismans. Remember the Albert Schweitzer cardigan that someone bought for him when he came over to England on a visit and which he left behind when he returned to Africa saying he had no need of it there? You wore that cardigan in so many English films including *A Married Man*, the last thing you worked on. David had that and Jake had the red cashmere. Dad was given the lovely sports jacket that you bought the previous year and said that he felt like a millionaire in it. I'm glad that he wasn't around during all the proceedings. You know that his cancer was in remission – well, sadly it returned in the New Year and he died in March, both my supports gone together. It was a grim time, darling. The famous jacket then passed on to David.

The funeral would have pleased you a lot: no godliness at all. Gerry Parrot presided. I met him through Diana when you were in King's College Hospital. She rushed me over to Southwark Cathedral one day when the mask slipped and I gave way to despair. 'I'm taking you to meet a Canon,' she said firmly. Well! Knowing what a heathen she is I was amazed, but he was just the person I needed. From then on he was always on the end of a phone to pep me up, and he supervised the funeral beautifully. He didn't object when I told him no prayers but snuck a bit of God into the committal, which no one noticed.

Derek Taylor wrote a marvellous piece about you with bits from your letters and lots of humour. Mark read it out for him in church. Dear Bill Pertwee told some wonderful stories. One was about a time when you travelled to Thetford together and you said, 'Let's go the pretty way and pat a few horses in Newmarket.' You decided to stop over, and when you got to the hotel there was only a twin-bedded room left, so you mucked in together. You went out for a curry dinner that night and in the small hours of the morning Bill woke up and found you sitting up in bed writing. 'What are you doing at this hour, John?' he said. 'I'm trying to put some lyrics to those dreadful noises you're making, dear boy,' you replied.

The church was full of laughter, although at the end of Bill's ovation, when he said, 'Apart from my family, I loved John more than anyone,' his voice broke. It was a touching moment. We chose some music you loved, the score to *Monsieur Hulot's Holiday* which the BBC dug out and sent to me as a tribute to you. It hit just the right laid-back feeling when we entered, like we were just 'hanging out'. We had Annie Ross singing 'What's New?' of course, and a piece by Alan Clare that you liked called 'John – O'Groats', then a recording of your voice saying the Indian prayer that you loved.

When I am dead cry for me a little.
Think of me sometimes
But not too much.

Think of me now and again as I was in life,
At some moment it is pleasant to recall.
But not for long.

Leave me in peace, and I shall leave you in
    peace,
And while you live let your thoughts be
    with the living

Which was a complete stab in the stomach
and made me cry, which I had tried so hard
not to do. We left you with spring from
Vivaldi's 'Four Seasons', which pulled us
together.

We had tried to keep it private, just family
and friends, everyone *you* loved, but the
gentlemen of the press were there hiding
behind bushes in their sheepskins looking
like a bunch of flashers, and the most extraordinary thing, a couple of complete
strangers who were in the waiting room
when we arrived; we thought they were early
for the next funeral but they came right into
the church with us. It turned out that a
distant aunt by marriage had told them to
come. I hope that they were suitably
shocked and embarrassed. (Imagine gate-
crashing a funeral.)

I picked out the undertakers, a Mr and
Mrs Love, from the phone book. Who else
with a name like that? They did a fine job
and Mr Love said that it was the funniest yet

most touching funeral he'd ever arranged. Although I had specified no flowers, saying that donations should go to CND or animal charities, there were lots of blooming tributes, one from Rod Stewart and the boys and of course one from Robin who came to visit with Bunny soon after the tour ended.

As a final touch David and Jake had got an inner tube and covered it with leaves and put it on our front door when we got back home, in memory of your favourite scene from *Monsieur Hulot's Holiday* for anyone who was in on the joke. (It was well known that Jacques Tati who created Monsieur Hulot was John's idol. He could also do a fair impersonation of his walk.)

Bruce Copp had made a gourmet buffet and those who didn't drink assembled in your bedroom for an illegal smoke. It was quite a party with so many lovely stories about you from all your friends. Annie Ross and I sang 'Sleeping Bee' from *House of Flowers* as we had done every time we met, and you were truly honoured.

Here's a letter from Derek Taylor about the day.

My dear Joan,

Wild! What a funeral…

It was wonderful to see you all yesterday and a privilege to share in the tribute to the great one.

I was so glad to meet 'the grown up boys'* and don't want to lose sight of everyone again. So, thank you Joan dear for such a day when it might have been something else entirely. The train, within eight minutes of leaving you all, was *surreal*, not a word I use lightly. Some of what Neil Kinnock calls 'seed-corn' (modern youth) lifted my newspaper as I was reading the back, and read the front page aloud, tugging at it to get to the next line. I was feeling so benign that I smiled at them and they accepted me as a sort of co-owner of the paper, rather than resenting me for hanging on to it. It could have been a very off-the-wall commercial for the *Guardian*. They got out at Herne Bay in a flurry of profanity and cigarette smoke.

* And grown-up girls.

The 21st century promises to be 'A Lot Of Fun'.

The piece that Mark read out with such deceptive ease will follow under plain cover, when properly set up either in type or here at this machine. I must congratulate you all on carrying the ball forward so well. I will *never* forget it, I say, as if I too were going to live forever.

Invidious to mention names, but so many yesterday were such good fun, very touching in unison for the event, but very *different* folk. My God, what a cast! No playwright, not the great Alan Bennett, not Pinter (well maybe him, yes) in sunny mood could have put that lot, us lot, together.

I hope you can push ahead OK Joan … I'm sure you can. Such spirit!

Keep in touch. Good luck with the book. Brook no argument.

Oh… The Ramsgate developers and juggernauts! Do you want me to put the dogs of war at the BBC and ITV on to it, *if* they will bite?

Love

Derek xx

When the guests had left I thanked God for having a family to draw around me at such a time and thought what it must be like for poor souls who have no one.

During the following weeks I was mercifully kept busy writing an epilogue to your book, which was due to be published in time for Christmas. It was a rushed job for the publishers as you had inconveniently departed so unexpectedly and I had to buckle down and write for the first time in my life. It came quite quickly. I was still full of memories and there were so many stories.

As I had no typewriter and wouldn't have been able to use one if I had, I obtained the services of a very proper lady from a respectable local secretarial agency to put down my scribble and also to type out my letters of thanks to all the people who had sent their condolences.

One of the stories I related for your book was the tale of the Sunday we went to London by train for the day and everything went wrong on good old British Rail, so I'll jog your memory by repeating it.

When we got to Ramsgate station we were told that we would have to disembark a few stops up the line at Herne Bay and board a bus, which would take us to Faversham to pick up the London train, thereby adding a considerable length of time to the journey, which you hated anyway. It was a family joke that every time you arrived by train from London, your opening remark was always, 'I've just had the most awful journey of my life.'

You said in your book that when you went to school in Birchington (a few stops from Ramsgate) at the age of eight, the journey took two hours and still does to this day. But I digress. When told by the jolly train guard that this bus journey would take place you said, 'Oh Lor' or something similar and he replied, 'With your money, John, you could afford to hire a helicopter...' 'No comment,' you said. As we boarded the train you said, 'I wonder if it will get any worse.' 'What?' I asked. 'The fucking day,' you answered despairingly. When we were leaving the station at Herne Bay to get on the bus we passed a poster of Jimmy Savile with a cheeky expression on his face giving the thumbs up. 'Let the train take the strain,' it cheerily advised us. 'Cunt,' you said.

As this lady who was doing my typing was well spoken and refined, I was loath to offend her and warned her that there would be a couple of four-letter words in the script that were essential to the plot and I hoped that she wouldn't be too shocked by them.

'My goodness, Mrs Le Mesurier, my father was an admiral,' she said, 'so I'm no stranger to lower-deck expletives.'

Reassured I began my dictation, 'fucking' slipped by without a hitch and I thought 'cunt' had followed also without affront but a sentence later she said, 'This word cunt, Mrs Le Mesurier, how do you spell it?' 'C-U-N-T,' I said nervously. 'Well it's a new one to me,' she said. 'What exactly does it mean?' I thought she might have been pulling my leg, but the light of innocence in her guileless blue eyes convinced me otherwise. 'Well,' I said, 'it means being a silly Billy.'

From then on Derek Taylor, to whom I related the tale with great glee, used it regularly in his letters to me, which incidentally continued until he died. And it was a household expression in the family. 'Oh don't be such a silly Billy dear,' we would say.

When your book was published there was no one to do the publicity but me. As I had never been interviewed on film, radio or in the press, it was a scary experience. I went on *Woman's Hour* and was so scared that my voice came over like a whisper and my brain refused to remember any part of our life together, so I must have been thought of as deadly dull.

I was by then getting a kickback from your death as is normal in bereavement. For a while there had been so much to do for instance, planning your memorial service at the actors' church in Covent Garden occupied my time for a while. It had to be just right on the same lines as your funeral with the emphasis on laughter and music. So many people wanted to speak about you that it was hard to refuse them. But as there was only so much time allowed for your tribute, and so much to say, some of it had to be left out. Nevertheless I insisted that Bill Pertwee repeated his speech from the funeral, and Mark the wonderful piece that Derek Taylor had written which showed, through your letters, the sort of man you were.

Needless to say, the church was packed. Standing room at the back and lots of people left outside. The press were there in abundance but this time it was a public tribute so I didn't mind. The next day my picture was on the front page of several newspapers. I was laughing and the caption said, 'In Laughing Memory', and all of them stressed how such a doleful and apparently melancholy man could have one of the funniest send-offs. How you would have loved it all.

However, the slump came soon after, when all the kids went back to their every-day lives. Robin and Bunny, Jake, David, Susie and Emma, friends such as Annie Ross, Diana and Mark, Peter Campbell all had their own things to do. And without you with me each day to care for and talk to and cook for, I didn't have a direction or at times a reason for getting up. To make matters worse I lost Nichodemus our beloved cat. He just vanished one day. He could have been stolen as, despite by then only having one eye and crooked whiskers and in general being about the ugliest looking cat in catdom, we knew he was a very rare Burmese Rex and apparently the first brown one ever to be reared. He had been given to us by an American woman. You remember Ferle Foxmarten, who wanted a cute little cat and got Nicky who wanted attention twenty-four hours a day? He used to run up her legs when she came home from work in the evening and pounce on her as she slept which freaked her out, so she passed him on to us, to our great delight.

We had twelve years of him and so much laughter. He was accident prone, and lost the sight in one eye in a fight, which made him cross-eyed. His whiskers just snapped off as they grew; he had enormous ears and a long neck. Covered in tight astrakhan curls, he resembled a Walt Disney caricature. As the days passed without him and there was no word (only a few false leads as I had advertised a large reward in the local papers) my sorrow deepened and all the grief that I couldn't spill for you, manifested itself in my longing for that mangy looking and peculiar little cat. I still miss him and his loss is synonymous with yours; together you represented my stable happy life, now gone for ever. However, John darling, as my nature and my very slight brush with Buddhism were based on the optimistic belief that everything that happens *must* have a reason and must be used for growth, after a good old wallow in grief and self-pity I looked around the home where we had been so happy and realized that I would be the caretaker of a museum if I stayed on there with my memories. So I put it on the market and moved back into Grange Road.

Years later I bought my current home

nearby. It is another noble house, lightened and brightened by so many of your pictures and pieces. You'd be chuffed, I think, to see the two blue plaques fixed to the outside wall at the back, honouring both you and Tony and awarded very selectively by Comic Heritage. You also stand sentry outside the back door in a form of a small statue of Sergeant Wilson. I'm sure your presence has helped to make this a warm and happy home.

Mum and Dad had been living at Grange Road for several years, taking over the two top floors and installing a kitchen and bathroom but, with the recurrence of Dad's cancer had had to move to the ground floor, the stairs being too much for him. I moved into the top two floors, which they had vacated, and with the move my life began to shift and change in a direction that was eventually to be beyond my wildest imaginings.

As it had been with you, it now became the same with Dad; his illness took precedence over all else. I had begun driving lessons much to your dismay a year before and with your illness I had abandoned them, as you know. I can't imagine why you had such little faith in my driving, darling, but now I went back to it with a vengeance, spurred on by all my women friends, Diana and Susie particularly, who were both good drivers, Susie having taken advanced driving lessons years before. The venture was aided by my brother Terry, who had come from his home in America to be near Dad. Terry would take me to car parks and patiently put me through reversing and three-point turns and he was with me when I passed, to our great delight and Dad's. You would have been so proud of me, John, as from then on I was able to drive Dad to Canterbury for his radium treatment five days a week, and his chemotherapy, all of which he bore with cheerful stoicism. Sadly, Terry, who during his long visits would sit up with Dad throughout the night, was absent when he died.

A few months earlier a local doctor had suggested that Dad be put into a hospice for a rest and to get his drugs sorted out. Dad agreed eagerly, it would make a change, he said, although knowing him so well I suspected that it was to give Mum a rest.

John, I was so moved by the feeling of calm and love there that I had to go off for a weep; beauty and goodness always make me cry as you know. Dad loved it. His bed was always surrounded by nurses, whom he regaled with tales of his past and I'm sure he dropped your name once or a dozen times. He was so proud of having had you as a son-in-law. Remember when we told him we were getting married and he said to you, 'As long as you don't call me Dad, you can have her'?

One day, mother was waxing lyrical about the house and how happy they had been during their years there. Dad was obviously in pain but as usual kept it to himself. 'We've had the happiest days of our life in this house, haven't we, Fred?' she said brightly. 'That's right, as a matter of fact, I'm having one now,' he said looking at me with a grin. I burst into laughter. 'What have I said now?' Mum muttered. She was always unconsciously dropping wonderful mala-propisms. 'I've only got two pairs of hands,' she said once, and 'the trouble with antiques is they don't last.' On another occasion, once when we had let the top flat out, mother became worried about the amount of furniture the tenants were taking up-stairs. She caught them one day carrying a fridge up the stairs and accosted them with, 'I'll have you know, this house isn't a furniture suppository.'

After a couple of weeks away in the hospice, Dad wanted to come home. I think he knew that the end was near though he said nothing. The hospital had stopped all treatment, there was nothing left to do now but hope for a peaceful end and make every moment count. When Diana was sitting alone with him over a cup of tea one afternoon just before the end she asked if there was anything he needed. 'Diana, I'm a bloody millionaire,' Dad replied.

I bought a tape recorder so that Dad could put down his memories, which were so vivid and colourful they had to be captured. I would sit with him when Mum had gone to bed and prompt him to keep his life story in context. It was riveting and as clear as yesterday to him. I felt as if I had a ringside seat as his earliest recollections unfolded. And I knew and loved the child he had been and the man that he was.

One morning the intercom system that we had installed between our flats buzzed frantically. I rushed downstairs to find that Dad had begun to haemorrhage from his mouth, so I rang the doctor who sent an ambulance to take him back to the hospice. He fell into a coma and when I saw him later that day the swelling had gone and his face was calm and peaceful. Beside him on the pillow someone had placed a small bunch of anemones, his favourite flowers. Two years later on a spring morning when my life had taken on an entirely new direction and I was living in a small town in Spain, I was walking home from the local market, carrying a heavy shopping bag in one hand and a small bunch of anemones in the other. As I put my hands up to my shoulder to stop the shopping bag from slipping I saw my dad's face flash before me with the anemones on the pillow. It came without reason triggered by the flowers. As I came through the door of my cottage the phone rang, it was Bruce Copp telling me that he had just looked through his diary, and found that it was the anniversary of Dad's death.

Dear John, what a sad phase of my life it all was, but I had had it so good for so long that things had been very one-sided. So there we were, Mum and I together in the same house, two widows bereaved within a few months of each other. If we hadn't had our separate apartments it could have been difficult: Mum being a bossy old Leo, as tough and masculine as my Dad had been, she ruled the roost and had moods that had to be humoured or else. Once when David was young he brought me a cup of tea up one morning and said, 'She's being a dying grandmother this morning.' I used to call them her Welsh witch moods and you and I would give her a wide berth when they descended. Do you remember how she used to change the London Road house around when we went away? It was beautifully clean and cared for and Dad would keep my garden in trim but Mum always wanted to put her stamp on it. It drove you mad if she moved a painting. Remember that sexy Henry Bardon nude that you bought, of a woman astride a man having a lovely time? At first, you don't notice him as she's so beautiful, then you realize why she's smiling! Well, Mum always covered it with a tea towel during our absence, and on your return you would tear it off with a flourish and a string of your colourful expletives.

That spring after your death I became an activist. Ramsgate council, in their wisdom, had decided to put a road to the harbour – which was becoming a freight port as opposed to a passenger ferry – right under and around Pegwell Bay, one of our favourite places. We used to love a brisk walk to the Bellevue Pub on the cliff where we would sit in the garden and watch the light on the sea. It enraged me to see it threatened so I wrote a letter to the local newspaper saying that I was going to withhold my rates as I did not want my money used this way and urged other ratepayers to do the same. I used your name shamelessly to shine a light on the matter as I have done on many occasions since and the press always rally, their pieces usually beginning with *Dad's Army* Widow etc. on this occasion the headline read '*Dad's Army* Widow Risks Prison By Refusing To Pay Her Rates'. Diana joined the fight and the town was divided between anti- and pro-road lobbies.

There were meetings with lots of raised voices and two old harpies rounded on Diana and me as we left one of them, calling us a couple of out-of-town tarts who ought to go back where we came from. It was great fun and it helped me through that sad time having something to fight for.

Our kindly vulture of the press, however, pulled a nasty trick on me by ringing up to get a statement about the road protest, which I gladly gave him for a good twenty minutes. He ended by asking me in an off-the-record manner if I had sold my London Road house because it was too big or be-

cause I needed the money. He had interviewed you once at London Road for a
magazine. I fell right into the trap and said
that I needed the money. 'But John must
have left you well provided for,' he said
sympathetically. I told him that the pay of a
jobbing actor was unsteady and never all
that good and that actors were only paid
when they worked, there was no unemploy-
ment benefit for you when you were not
working. Also, doing a cameo appearance in
a film could often mean only about a day or
even half a day's work.

I chatted on trustingly and a couple of
days later in the *Daily Mirror* there was a
half-page article headed, 'John left me
broke, said *Dad's Army* widow.' The piece
was worded as if you had left your money
elsewhere and that I was deliberately left out
of your will. His name was Bill Evans, like
your favourite jazz pianist so it stuck in my
memory. I tracked him down and gave him
a piece of my mind but have never trusted
journalists since because of it. What hurt
was that it was the only unpleasant thing
that had been written with regard to you.
How the vultures hover.

Anyway, the road protest burned itself out
in indifference. We led a parade around the

town with me at the front with a megaphone saying 'Wake up, Ramsgate, save your town,' with little Emma beside me echoing whatever I said. I made two TV appearances; the second was outside the courtroom at Ramsgate where I was threatened, not with prison, which I was rather looking forward to out of curiosity, but with a visit from the bailiffs, which would have been pointless, and not newsworthy.

Well John, seventeen years later Ramsgate got its road by which time the freight port is barely used and the passenger ferry service, which would have been an asset to Ramsgate, has ceased to exist. As usual Ramsgate is consumed with apathy. Remember the funny letter you wrote to the local paper about the clocks? How every public clock in town was either stopped or wrong? Sadly, I've lost the cutting. Then there was the time you opened an exhibition of Ralph Hoult's collection of old prints of Ramsgate and the mayor was there with some of his council members. When you stood up to make a speech about your love of the town, you said, 'I would like to begin by talking about dog shit.' I got the giggles and so did you. You were mischievous at times, John, after all the years we were together you always managed to surprise me. Do you remember coming to see *Godspell*, which I had seen three times and adored? You said that it was one of the most embarrassing experiences of your life and hated every moment. Mind you, I was a bit of a hippy in those days. I had come to it all very late on; you called me the middle-aged hippy and would have none of it but we both got on with our own lives and did not seem to clash in any great degree.

Dear John, in the summer of 1984 I went to visit Bruce Copp in Spain. He had moved there a year before and was living in a hill village called La Floresta in Catalonia just above Barcelona. He loved the life and had made many local friends, acquired several animals and become a dedicated gardener. The change was exactly what I needed; it was light years away from Ramsgate and all the memories. While there he took me to see Sitges, a small town just along the coast from Barcelona. He drove me through the pretty streets of the old town and parked outside the church, which looked down at the town and promenade. It was the most beautiful introduction to the town and as I leaned over the wall and looked down at it I fell in love and wanted it more than anything else in the world. We stayed there for two days and during that time I visualized myself as part of it all, doing the market, getting to know the people and worming my way into a completely new way of life. By the time the two days were up I had decided to come back for a year, a sabbatical.

To cut a very long story short, Sitges wrapped itself around me and I planted my heart there for seven healing years.

I was not lonely because everybody came to visit: David and Susie, Jake, Emma, who adored it, even Mum came regularly, as did all my friends. Mark and his third wife, Susie Nichols, came for a visit, fell in love with it and bought a holiday apartment there. With his help and Bruce's, and Bunny's, I raised enough money to buy a huge ancient house in a narrow cobbled street just by the beach.

I opened a guesthouse for thespians and cats and actually got paid for doing something I had always enjoyed, cooking and having company. I met some wonderful new friends and all the old ones came out for breaks. The cats didn't pay, although they acted as if they owned the place. In my prospectus, in which I shamelessly pulled strings, I called in old favours and evoked your beloved name, sending it to all the TV studios and agents, also to friends to hand out. I stated that the guests must love cats and even be prepared to sleep with them.

I ran it like a house party, and at times the casting was bizarre to say the least. One week I had at the same time a Rasta pop star, his girlfriend, his manager, an actor friend of Jake's and his wife. She was a punk rocker with clouds of screaming pink hair, and there was a gay writer and his boy-friend. Also a TV presenter from Granada called Barbara McDonald, who had looked at the notice board at work hoping to find a mountain bike, but instead she found me. She's now my best friend. Also into the gathering came an elderly couple on their first visit to Spain, recommended by my friend Sheila. He had just retired from a lifetime of drudgery in ladies underwear and was flexing his wings of freedom. Their faces on entering the house and being con-fronted by this human clash of colour was a study, as they say. It was the hour before dinner when everyone was in the dining-room pouring drinks and chatting in the kitchen as I cooked. In a couple of seconds their faces registered fear, suspicion, doubt and curiosity but they were welcomed warmly by one and all and ended by being charmed.

Often I visualized you sitting at the head of the long dinner table holding court and soaking up the atmosphere, and I had the strong feeling that you would have approved of all the comings and goings in my new life. Jake lived with me for four good years, and he was happy during that time. He was popular in the town, his musician's ear quickly picked up the language, even Catalan. He became a sort of odd-job man, and (unlike his father), able to fix things when the plumbing went wrong or the lights failed. All the guests loved him, lots of them were his friends, hence the mixture of musicians and thespians.

However, darling, things change. Mother developed the early stages of Alzheimer's. When the chimney fell in, I admitted to myself that the house in Calle Taco had begun to crumble and England, home and duty were calling.

It was hard to leave but everything has its time and it was time to go home. So far, thanks largely to you and the examples you set just by being your true and gentle self, my life has seemed charmed and protected, your love still gives me the confidence to

338

know who I am and where I'm going. In fact I'm moving on again soon. I have bought an old ruin in Portugal, which is being restored. I will be near the Dunns and life seems sweet there.

I'll end by saying that one of my most used expressions as I go through life is, 'How John would have loved this.' And I hope that when my times comes I can say as you did.

'It's all been rather lovely.'

It certainly has so far.

Love *Joan*

P.S. Just after I finished my letter to you I was invited to a weekend in Thetford to commemorate the opening of the Dad's Army Museum at Bressingham Steam Museum. It was a gala occasion, ticket sales had doubled their expectation, and Bill Pertwee said that all of those invited would be given bodyguards from the army volunteer service to protect us as on the last reunion he and Frank Williams were knocked off the fire engine by over enthusiastic fans. Can you picture it? I drove up from Ramsgate picking up Clive Dunn and Kay Beck, Jimmy's widow, on the way.

On the Friday afternoon I drove to Bury St Edmunds to see the old house where you spent your childhood and dreamed your dreams. It was as lovely as you described in a peaceful square, and I saw you there so clearly having a sort of John Betjeman life and flirting with a succession of Joan Hunter Dunns. There seemed to be nobody at home, the shutters on one side of the house were closed, not that I would have been bold enough to knock and expect to be invited inside, but how I would have loved to. I did peep through the drawing-room window into an elegant panelled room and imagined you having a glass of sherry with Mummy at the age of six, as you once jokingly told me you did, and over the garden wall at the side I caught a glimpse of laburnum – you always talked of the beautiful laburnum trees.

That evening at the Bell Inn they held a dinner for all the remaining cast, friends, old wives and members of the *Dad's Army* appreciation society who had arranged the following day's festivities, and a room had been set aside for us. They had laid too many places, not knowing how many would be present. It was a lovely evening of reminiscences and laughter. Lots of speeches were made and glasses were raised frequently in your honour.

We sat at a big square table and when we counted the empty seats, there were six, one for each of you no longer with us. It was quite unplanned, sheer coincidence but it gave us all a strange feeling and raised the hairs on the back of our necks to think that you were all looking in on us and sharing the moment.

I hope you were.

Much love, from

Joan

When I asked Clive Dunn if he had received any letters from John, he said that as they were so often together, there had not been any need to correspond and he could only remember sending a postcard when John was in hospital asking him not to die and to get better quickly.

So this is to John in heaven in which he remembers all the years of their friendship.

Dear John,

    It seems a hundred years and better,
Since I wrote you a little letter,
And asked you not to die,
But you disobediently did, and made me
  cry
Not half but all of us!
And then we had to laugh because of you,
And since it's been laughter every after.

Recently they hung a plaque, a plaque
  would you believe? Above your door
I know we should've mailed you
On the day that we unveiled you
But I know that you'd have found it such a
  bore!

John Le Mesurier a gent
Slightly Camp but never bent,
Actor laddie tale unfurls,
Off to work to please the girls,

One day did two double takes
For standing there was Hattie Jacques,
Married her good luck god bless!
Creaking beds at Eardley Cres,
You did some plays with quite short runs
Hattie gave you two nice sons

(I don't know why I'm writing this you'll
   read it and you'll take the piss).

One of your best friends was Polly,
Six years old and very jolly
Waiting by the windowsill,
Waiting patiently until
'He's here, he's here, here comes poor John
Put the gin and tonic on!'

From Brook Green you did arrive
Out of breath and sixty-five,
Ambled through the garden gate
Crooked smile and rather late,
Polly told you bed-time tales
Horror time with ghastly wails
Sticky hand on your hand tightened
Then you had to look quite frightened,
I see you now, not long after
Head thrown back in silent laughter.

You loved golf and other tosh
Good straight bat, a dab at squash.
Every old film that we see, switch it on and
   'there you'd be'
Believable as brave or funk
Sometimes blubbing
Sometimes drunk,
Hippie vicar, army gent,

You did them all to pay the rent,
Generous with what you got
Then spent the rest at Ronnie Scott,
Ah! Ronnie Scott's quite late at night
Fag in mouth and nicely tight.
The jazz club where you could unbend,
Where every man was your best friend
Another scotch another joint
Hum a tune and make a point of paying
   bills and never shout
Last man in last man out!

Off to work, John, show a leg
Couldn't boil a fucking egg.
Love a cat and love a pup
Hacking jacket cuffs turned up.

Meeting Joan now that was handy
Very succulent and randy
Sometimes running out of view
Round the bend but still loved you
Grown up people make amend
Now you had a real best friend.

Both of you survived rough weather
Travelled here and there together;
Remember when you stayed awhile
On a sunny Spanish isle?
Remember sitting on a rock

Then tied a ribbon round your cock!
And shouted at a passing fan
God bless you merry gentleman!
(I only wrote that for a thrill, I'm sure that
  tales apocryphal)

You kindly said you'd like to slaughter
Little boys who shout near water,
'Clear off you boys,' you bravely cried,
Then all the little boys replied
'We're not breaking any laws
Since when as this canal been yours?'
Then one young boy who stood out front
Said 'you clear off, white haired old ★★★★!'
Then screaming shouting off they run
Now *that* was your idea of fun.

I recall on tour you took me racing
'Give those bookmakers a lacing!'
You knew the tipster, tip was hot,
Then you lost the bleeding lot,
Drown the sorrow, habits chronic
Have another gin and tonic.

I could write on a mile or more,
You'd only say 'God what a bore!'
You see to *me*, you're still alive

Wish you were

With love from

Clive

The publishers hope that this book has given you enjoyable reading. Large Print Books are especially designed to be as easy to see and hold as possible. If you wish a complete list of our books please ask at your local library or write directly to:

Magna Large Print Books
Magna House, Long Preston,
Skipton, North Yorkshire.
BD23 4ND

Other MAGNA Titles
In Large Print

ANNE BAKER
Merseyside Girls

JESSICA BLAIR
The Long Way Home

W. J. BURLEY
The House Of Care

MEG HUTCHINSON
No Place For A Woman

JOAN JONKER
Many A Tear Has To Fall

LYNDA PAGE
All Or Nothing

NICHOLAS RHEA
Constable Over The Bridge

MARGARET THORNTON
Beyond The Sunset